THE CREATION OF WEALTH

David D. Miller
1985

THE CREATION OF WEALTH

Brian Griffiths

HODDER AND STOUGHTON
LONDON SYDNEY AUCKLAND TORONTO

British Library Cataloguing in Publication Data

Griffiths, Brian, *1941–*
The creation of wealth.–(Hodder
Christian paperbacks)
1. Wealth—Religious aspects—
Christianity
I. Title
261.8'34 BR115.W4

ISBN 0-340-35543-3

 Printed in Great Britain for Hodder and Stoughton Limited, Mill Road, Dunton Green, Sevenoaks, Kent by Richard Clay (The Chaucer Press) Limited, Bungay, Suffolk. Photoset by Rowland Phototypesetting Limited, Bury St Edmunds, Suffolk. Hodder and Stoughton Editorial Office: 47 Bedford Square, London WC1B 3DP.

To Aeronwen

CONTENTS

ACKNOWLEDGMENTS

This book has been written at the invitation of the Christian Association of Business Executives (CABE), as part of a project on the creation of wealth. I am grateful for all the comments which I have received from members of the Association, but my greatest debt is due to its Director, Hugh Kaye, in particular, for his constant encouragement and his readiness to help in so many ways. I am indebted both to the Association and to the Colt Foundation for the financial support which has made the project possible.

I would also like to thank David Bell for acting as Research Assistant during part of the study and to Rachel Steare for acting as editor and making numerous suggestions for improvements in the text and footnotes as well as ensuring that the notes and index were properly prepared. I am grateful to Andrew Chambers, Geoffrey Wood, Forrest Capie, Alan Peters and Alan Vickery for reading a first draft of the manuscript and making many useful comments. Finally I would like to thank Agatha Bobb and Elaine Levine for typing the manuscript.

1

INTRODUCTION

The Christian Church has never found it easy to come to terms with the market place. Ever since the early Church's experiment in communism there have always been those who have considered that private property, interest and profit were at best questionable and at worst immoral and wicked. Among the Church Fathers, Origen criticised anyone who did not take literally the words of Christ and sell his possessions and give to the poor. From the fourth to the sixteenth century the General Councils of the Church repeatedly condemned usury as something detestable and shameful. In the mid-nineteenth century the emergence of Christian Socialism was a response to the alleged selfishness and human indignity of the system of *laissez faire* which had grown up with the Industrial Revolution. Earlier in this century T. S. Eliot contrasted a commercial society with a Christian society, arguing that 'the organisation of society on the principle of private profit, as well as public destruction, is leading both to the deformation of humanity by unregulated industrialisation, and to the exhaustion of natural resources; and a great deal of our material progress for which succeeding generations may have to pay dearly'.[1]

Since medieval times, however, views such as these have been held by a relatively small number of Christian theologians and clergymen. What distinguishes the last quarter of a century is the way in which a trickle has grown into a flood. If one examines the sermons, speeches, writings and conference resolutions of contemporary churchmen the overwhelming impression one receives is of a deep hostility to the market economy, the pursuit of profit, privately owned property and, that most characteristic institution of modern capitalism, the privately owned corporation.

For example, E. F. Schumacher in his stimulating book *Small is Beautiful*, after observing that in the market place transactions depend on market value and not the intrinsic qualities of the goods themselves, concludes that 'the market is the institutionalisation of individualism and non-responsibility. Neither buyer nor seller is responsible for anything but himself.'[2] In his famous Encyclical Letter *Popolorum Progressio* (*The Great Social Problem*), Pope Paul VI, after applauding the process of industrialisation, laments the development of liberal capitalism. 'It is unfortunate that . . . a system has been constructed which considers profit as the key motive for economic progress, competition as the supreme law of economics and private ownership of the means of production as an absolute right that has no limits and carries no corresponding social obligations. This unchecked liberation leads to dictatorship rightly denounced by Pius XI as producing "the international imperialism of money."'[3] Miguez Bonino, the respected Protestant theologian from Argentina, in a distinguished series of lectures given in London in 1974, is equally outspoken: 'The basic ethos of capitalism is definitely anti-Christian: it is the maximizing of economic gain, the raising of man's grasping impulse, the idolizing of the strong, the subordination of man to the economic production. Humanisation is for capitalism an unintended by-product . . . Solidarity is for capitalism accidental.'[4]

The number of examples which might be given are enormous. But in all, the general theme is perfectly clear. It is that a market economy, which is dependent on the institution of private property and a system of competitive markets, which allows profits to be the criterion for survival and which encourages freedom of individual choice, results in a competitive, greedy, unequal and materialistic society which runs totally counter to the teachings of Jesus on these subjects. Because materialism, exploitation and injustice are built into the very structures of the market place the Christian who wishes to be true to his faith therefore has no option but to reject the whole system. This places the businessman in an intolerable position because it implies that he is either corrupt or naive. If these criticisms are correct, then there is no way in which a public-spirited individual can make a career in business and remain a person of integrity.

The moral problem, however, is more complicated than this. It so happens that as a matter of history it was the market economy which brought about the transformation of the Western world from widespread poverty to the level of prosperity which it now enjoys. In the mid-eighteenth century, life in England was comparable to that in many Third World countries today: low real income, little education, poor housing, widespread disease and short life expectancy. By the end of the nineteenth century, the situation had changed dramatically. Real incomes had quadrupled, education was widespread, the housing stock had grown dramatically and life expectancy had increased. In no small measure this was due to the ability of the market economy to harness the inventiveness and entrepreneurial resources of ordinary people. The same progress took place in Western Europe, North America, Australia and New Zealand and once again within the context of free enterprise and small government involvement.

Just as important as the historic development of the West is the situation today. Wherever we look in the modern world we find that market economies create wealth more efficiently than state-owned and state-planned economies. If we compare the First World market-oriented economies with the Second World of socialist systems, then despite the relative economic stagnation of capitalist countries since the Vietnam War, real per capita consumption is far higher in these countries than in socialist ones. If we compare the economic performance of the Third World countries which rely on free enterprise – countries such as Malaysia, Hong Kong and South Korea – with those that rely on state enterprise – such as Tanzania, Mozambique and India – those oriented to the market economy tend to be more productive and prosperous than those oriented towards state planning and substantial government regulation.[5]

If the nations of the world were uninterested in wealth creation, the fact that market economies tend regularly to outperform socialist economies would be of no consequence. But the countries of the Second and Third Worlds are desperately concerned to improve their standards of living. In introducing the 1979 World Development Report, Robert S. McNamara stated that 'Over the next two decades, these countries will face unprecedented challenges: they will need to create productive employment for a work force that is likely to expand by more than 500 million people between 1975 and 2000; over the same period their cities will need to provide jobs, housing, transportation, water, sanitation and health care for almost one billion additional inhabitants.'[6]. Even in the relatively affluent Western countries there is widespread demand for better housing, better schools and better hospitals, a more generous system of social welfare benefits as well as improved transport and improved capabilities of national defence. The reduction of poverty in Third World countries and the provision of better housing, health, education and welfare in industrialised countries depends on industrialised countries themselves achieving a far more rapid rate of wealth creation than is taking place at present.

The case for a certain amount of redistribution through an anti-poverty programme is a strong one, but redistribution on the scale now being demanded would not solve the fundamental problems of our societies or our world. First, the possibilities for raising incomes in Third World countries by this route, even if we allow for the most radical redistribution of income and wealth, are more limited than is often assumed. Second, a good deal of wealth in the West is embodied in a highly skilled labour force, so that it is impossible to transfer high-technology industry to less developed countries without at the same time transferring high-technology personnel as well. Third, an attempted redistribution on the necessary scale would reduce the West itself to poverty. Unless the redistribution were voluntary, it could only be achieved by taxation. But involuntary taxation of this magnitude would be a major disincentive to wealth creation in Western countries. If the problem of domestic or global poverty were to be tackled by a strategy of redistributive taxation, it would simply be a prescription for greater misery for all. Fourth, redistribution through the coercive power of the state breeds dependence. The creation of the welfare state in developed countries has bred a new class which is to a greater or lesser extent dependent on the state for employment, education, health, housing, benefits, security and status. In Third World countries, the same dependency syndrome has appeared. If food is brought in, why produce it? If bureaucracy can profit from handing out aid, why encourage domestic production? If personal wealth can be obtained through holding political office, why bother to set up new enterprises? If agricultural output must be sold to a government monopoly buying agency, why bother to innovate and seek out new markets? Finally, advocates of international redistribution of wealth seldom address themselves to the question of the mechanisms by which this would be accomplished. A global welfare state would require a global coercive government with powers to enforce taxation measures akin to those now exercised by nation states, assuming (not unreasonably) that the West would be unwilling to surrender its 'surplus' wealth voluntarily. The political, not to say, spiritual implications of such a development are immense.

The redistribution of wealth is not an adequate solution to the problem of world poverty. Continued emphasis on redistribution can only exacerbate the world's economic problems.

The problem we face can be stated as follows: market economies create wealth more efficiently than either state-owned or state-planned economies. It is true in developed countries; it is also true in developing countries. But many of the central features of market economies – competition, inequality, individualism – invoke widespread hostility on ethical grounds. For Christians, the emphasis of the market economy on profit, growth and prosperity seems to fit uncomfortably with what the gospels have to say on these subjects. More than that, it is widely held that capitalism as a system has produced such a materialistic way of life in the Western world that it now threatens to undermine Western societies in a way which might lead to their ultimate destruction.

This book is an attempt to tackle this problem. It does so by examining four dimensions of wealth creation. The next chapter deals with the economic dimension, and looks at the way in which wealth is created and the factors which are conducive to wealth creation. Then comes the theological dimension: does wealth creation play any part in the message of the gospels? After that we consider various ethical objections to a system of markets and finally we look at the ideological dimension, and explore the extent to which the market economy can be rescued from a secular humanist philosophy. Its conclusion is that within a Christian perspective, the process of wealth creation has legitimacy and that while the Christian gospel cannot and should not be used to baptise any historical economic system, the market economy offers a better starting point than most other systems as well as providing an enormous opportunity for Christians in business to create structures at work which are authentically Christian.

2

THE ECONOMIC DIMENSION

The Crisis of Wealth Creation in the Western World

For the past decade the West has faced a crisis over wealth creation. Until the late sixties, the post-Second World War years proved to be a period of sharply rising prosperity and stability. Inflation was low, productivity and growth were high, unemployment was at lower levels than was ever thought possible before the Second World War and trade between nations was increasing at the same time as trade barriers and foreign exchange controls were being dismantled. But in the late sixties something curious happened. Since that time the situation has changed and it would not be too strong to say that from then onwards the Western world has been in a state of continuous economic crisis. A number of major factors have been at work.

Most wars in history have been followed by *inflation*, and the Vietnam War was no exception. In order to pay for the war, President Johnson printed money and government bonds, rather than raise taxes. The result was inflation. And because countries were linked together by a system of fixed exchange rates, and the dollar was the world's money, the US inflation was transmitted throughout the Western world. Since that time, central banks have continued to print money in an excessive and unpredictable fashion with the result that inflation has remained high and variable throughout industrial countries.

But high and variable rates of inflation have meant uncertainty for business over wage costs, interest rates and profit levels and therefore a reluctance to lay out capital for expansion.

A second factor, and one partly caused by the first, was the decision of the oil-producing countries to quadruple *the price of oil* and cut its supply in 1973–4 and then again to double its price and reduce its supply further in 1979–80. The oil-price shocks have had a major impact on Western economies – in raising prices, reducing output and transferring wealth from oil-consuming to oil-producing countries. At the same time, the possibility that OPEC might do the same again led to continued uncertainty over growth and inflation in industrialised countries with further ramifications for the cost of capital and exchange rates.

Rising inflation has also been accompanied by *rising unemployment*. In the fifties and early sixties it used to be thought that there was a negative trade-off between inflation and unemployment – unemployment could be reduced but only at the cost of higher rates of inflation. Policy-makers were therefore confronted with a menu of choice – they could choose the desired level of inflation or of unemployment but not both. Since the mid-sixties, however, the situation has deteriorated.

The third major factor has been the *growth of government*. Between 1961 and 1981 total government expenditure as a percentage of gross domestic product rose dramatically in most Western countries. For example, in the United Kingdom it rose from 33.4 per cent to 47.3 per cent, in Germany from 33.8 per cent to 49.3 per cent, France from 35.7 per cent to 48.9 per cent, Italy from 29.4 per cent to 50.8 per cent, Canada from 30.0 per cent to 41.4 per cent, Belgium from 29.8 per cent to 56.11 per cent, Holland from 35.4 per cent to 61.5 per cent, and Sweden (the biggest government spender in the world) from 31.0 per cent to a staggering 65.3 per cent. In Japan it rose from 17.4 per cent to 34.0 per cent. The only real exception was the United States where between 1961 and 1981, it only rose from 29.0 per cent to 35.4 per cent.[1] In order to finance this higher expenditure, taxes and contributions such as national insurance as a percentage of gross domestic product have also risen in the same way.[2]

The combination of inflation, oil-price shocks and growing government has had a major impact on the performance of Western countries. Productivity has fallen unambiguously since the early 1970s. For example, productivity growth (measured by real gross national product in relation to civilian employment) for the United States between 1960 and 1973 averaged 2.1 per cent while between 1973 and 1980 it fell to −0.4 per cent; for Japan the figures were 9.1 per cent and 3.1 per cent; for Germany 4.5 per cent and 1.1 per cent; for the United Kingdom 3.0 per cent and −0.3 per cent; for Holland 4.0 per cent and −1.0 per cent; for Belgium 4.3 per cent and 0.6 per cent; and for Sweden 3.3 per cent and 1.3 per cent.[3] In addition, profitability has been reduced dramatically. The share of profits in domestic UK income fell from 15½ per cent in 1940–4 to 5½ per cent in 1974–7, with a sharp fall from 10½ per cent in 1970–3 to only 5 per cent in 1975.[4] Both pre- and post-tax rates of return on trading assets and on capital have fallen more or less consistently over the past twenty years. In 1963 the pre-tax real rate of return on trading assets was 11.4 per cent. By 1975 this had fallen to 5.2 per cent. After recovering slightly to 7.2 per cent in 1978, it fell to only 2.7 per cent in 1981, the lowest ever recorded.[5]

The economic crisis in the West over the past two decades is frequently described and analysed in purely economic terms. Yet the past two decades have also witnessed profound changes in Western societies. In terms of economic life these years have seen a decline in moral standards. The growth in the black economy and tax evasion, the rise in pilfering from retail stores, the seriousness of employee theft and commercial fraud, the recent problems of Lloyds of London, all suggest changing standards.[6] At an everyday level, the growth of notices in shopping centres near large schools stating 'only two children are allowed in this shop at any one time' is characteristic of the seventies, not the fifties.

The changes in moral standards are not confined to economic life. The period of economic crisis has also been a period of rising crime, growing divorce rates, increasing illegitimacy and abortion, the acceptance of one-parent families as a norm, rapid growth in drug abuse and addiction, greater alcoholism and football hooliganism.[7] By contrast with the present, Professor Geoffrey Gorer, in a study examining the English character in 1955, claimed that the central problem for the understanding of society at that time was the remarkable degree of self-control over aggression exercised by its citizens.

> . . . in public life today, the English are certainly among the most peaceful, gentle, courteous and orderly populations that the civilised world has ever seen. But from the psychological point of view this is still the same problem; the control of aggression when it has gone to such remarkable lengths that you hardly ever see a fight in a bar (a not uncommon spectacle in most of the rest of Europe or the USA), when football crowds are as orderly as church meetings . . . this orderliness and gentleness, this absence of overt aggression calls for an explanation if the dynamics of English character are to be effectively described.[8]

The fascinating question raised by the coincidence of these trends is their interrelationship and the extent to which they all reflect more deep-seated changes in the values of our society.

But first let us start with the economic dimension.

How Is Wealth Created?

The prosperity of an economy derives from two major sources: its resources and the efficiency with which they are used. Resources consist of natural endowments, people, intellectual know-how, consumer durables, plant and machinery and public utilities. The basic natural endowments include such things as land, fauna and flora, oil, gas and mineral deposits. The prosperity of Saudi Arabia depends on oil, South Africa on mineral deposits, Spain on beaches, Norway on trees and fish and Canada on the prairies. But resources need to be exploited. Mexico had oil in Aztec times, Australia had minerals before the settlers arrived, America had vast land before the West was opened up. The exploitation of natural resources requires that other resources – people, know-how, machines and the construction of public utilities such as roads, bridges and waterways – be involved.

The traditional way of categorising the resources of an economy is in terms of its factors of production – natural resources, labour and capital, with capital being those goods such as factories or machine tools or steel plants, which are used to produce other goods. This, however, is a very restricted concept of capital. If capital is defined as a stock of things which produces goods and services then we need to think in much broader terms.

The knowledge and skills of human beings are just as much a part of societies' capital as machines. Over the centuries human involvement in the production process has come to rely less and less on the use of brute force and more and more on the acquisition of skills and know-how. The person who supplies these in the labour market is therefore the owner of a valuable productive asset, which has been developed by investing time and real resources in training and which is expected to produce an increased income over time. It is this which justifies the expression 'human capital' being applied to labour and which confronts each supplier of labour with the same problems which confront any capitalist, namely what amount and what kind of investment to undertake.

The broader concept of capital also extends to the whole range of consumer durables: houses, cars, furnishings, kitchen equipment and clothes. A modern kitchen is as much a production unit as a traditional cottage industry. All consumer durables provide services without being used up immediately in the process. The broadest of all concepts of capital would include clean air and clean water, preservation of the environment and art collections. It is important to notice that capital as conventionally measured applies only to our initial and rather narrow definition. In terms of the definition we have given, the prosperity of an economy depends critically on its 'stock' of capital: physical, human, intellectual, environmental.

Historically it has been the accumulation of increasing amounts of capital, embodying as they did new technology, which raised dramatically the productivity of labour. The source of this increase in capital is saving: that is, it is income which is currently received but not consumed. An individual or a nation which consumes all of its current income is unable to build up capital. It is only when an individual or a society makes a conscious decision to forgo consumption that it is possible to accumulate capital. If a Robinson Crusoe living on a desert island devotes less time to catching fish and uses it to make a fishing net, he is enabled to accumulate capital, but only because he is prepared simultaneously to reduce his consumption of fish. Students who devote three years to study for a degree accept a lower standard of living for that time in order to increase their human capital and their future earning power. If the wages, tax payments and dividends of a corporation are less than its total revenue then it is enabled to increase its investment and add to its stock of net assets. If a nation consumes less than its total production of all goods and services in a particular year, resources are freed to enable the economy to build up its stock of capital. Capital only increases therefore through the process of saving.

It is important to notice that the act of saving always involves thinking beyond the present. Alfred Marshall, the distinguished Cambridge economist of the turn of the century, expressed it by saying that saving was associated with 'man's prospectiveness; that is, his faculty of realising the future'.[9] At the same time saving also implies less consumption. But less consumption always involves some element of sacrifice, self-denial or abstinence. This is true regardless of whether the economic system is capitalist or socialist. Under a capitalist system resources may be freed for capital accumulation by higher interest rates, whereas under a socialist regime the process may involve higher taxes, controls, rationing and forced saving. The mechanisms may differ in the two kinds of economies, but the basic principles that capital accumulation is dependent on saving, that saving involves taking account of the future, and that this process implies giving up something, are true in all economies at all times.

The creation of wealth takes place when an individual or corporation employs the potential labour and capital resources available and uses these to produce something (production is taken in the most general sense of the term) which has greater value than the resources used. In this sense wealth creation is the value added during the production process. For it to take place successfully a number of conditions must be met: the end product must have a monetary value greater than that of the resources drawn on; there must be some technical process of production; there has to be some person or group of people who take the entrepreneurial initiative in bringing the resources together; and there has to be some entity within which the whole process takes place – a family, partnership, company or public utility.

For it to take place at all it is necessary to understand first why the resources are prepared to be employed and second why it is that companies are prepared to employ them. Let us start with the company side. Companies are in business to make profit. The bottom line of the income and expenditure account is a measure of business success. Making profit will certainly not be the only reason why companies are in business but without a healthy profit, a business will be unable to survive. A company therefore will only hire more labour and borrow funds if it thinks that some unexploited profit opportunity exists. If it does not then, like GEC over recent years, it will accumulate highly liquid assets. (At present GEC is holding approximately £1000 million in cash.)[10] But it is also the prospect of material reward which at least partly motivates the suppliers of all resources involved in the production process.

So far we have avoided defining wealth; but we have come close to doing so more than once. In everyday language, wealth refers to the net assets or net worth of an individual, a family or a business. In this sense the meaning of wealth is close to that of capital. It is the stock of useful things owned by an individual, a family or corporation which yields a stream of income, either in cash or in kind. For an economy as a whole, wealth is more than the total capital stock, because it also includes that part of current income which has no capital source.

One thing which becomes immediately apparent from our approach is that there is no objective definition and measurement of wealth. By defining wealth as being made up of useful things, wealth depends on a process of valuation which by its very nature must be subjective. In a market economy the process of valuation depends on the preference and income of those who wish to buy and sell.

Within this framework we can see why the last decade has been so damaging to business and employment. The greater the uncertainty over the expected profit the less likely it is that a company will undertake capital expenditure. But inflation, volatile exchange rates, volatile interest rates, and oil-price shocks have been a direct cause of increasing uncertainty, as well as an indirect cause, because they prompt governments to take actions which are uncertain. In addition large government deficits and borrowing requirements have raised interest rates and made the cost of expansion and job creation that much higher. Public sector borrowing has crowded out private borrowing and with it private investment and job creation.[11] At the same time increased taxes on business and their employment of people, as well as employment-protection legislation, has driven a wedge between the cost to a firm of employing additional labour and the net take-home pay of the people being employed. This wedge has been increasing and is now very significant. Take, for example, the case of a family man earning £140 per week.

The extra cost to a company of employing such a person in terms of national insurance contribution and the cost of administration is roughly an extra 20 per cent. After the person has paid income tax, national insurance and the VAT and excise duties on purchases, the after-tax income is reduced roughly by 35 per cent. In other words, for a company to employ someone earning £140 per week costs the company £168 per week, yet the person receives only £105 per week. This wedge, which is a direct reflection of the size of government, is a major disincentive to employment.[12]

Wealth Creation – Three Historical Propositions

Before we examine the various factors which either hinder or help wealth creation, it is important to state three propositions about the subject, all of which have historical validity.

The first is that the primary source of wealth creation in the Western world over the past one hundred years has been the increasing efficiency with which resources are used rather than the growth of the resources themselves.

In other words, the major source of economic growth has not been a more rapid rate of investment or increased population growth but the improved efficiency of the way in which people, machines and buildings are being used in production.

A great deal of serious statistical research has been conducted on the economic growth of the West over the past one hundred years. The method employed has been to analyse the growth of total real national income in terms of the growth of inputs (labour, capital, land) and the growth of output per unit of input (productivity growth). Productivity growth occurs because of improvements in the quality of the inputs (more skilful labour force, new technology), the reaping of economies of scale from increased production (due to larger markets), and the removal or reduction of market imperfections (increased competition, lower trade barriers). Various studies have been made of this subject by, amongst others, Abramovitz, Cairncross, Dennison, Kuznets and Solow, and there is a remarkable similarity of conclusion among them. For example, a typical conclusion comes from Kuznets:

> While various modifications can be introduced into this statistical allocation, and while the results clearly vary among individual countries, the inescapable conclusion is that the direct contribution of man-hours and capital accumulation would hardly account for more than a tenth of the rate of growth in per capita product – and probably less. The large remainder must be assigned to an increase in efficiency in the productive resources – a rise in output per unit of input, due either to the improved quality of resources, or to the effects of changing arrangements, or to the impact of technological change, or to all three.[13]

The conclusions in this passage are common to all those cited above. What these writers are saying is that the economic growth of the West is not due primarily to capital growth, but to improvements in the quality of the labour force, better education, economies of scale and all those other factors which raise residual productivity.

This is a particularly important conclusion, because so many Third World countries seem to feel that if only they received a massive injection of capital, their economic performance would be transformed, that increased capital would automatically bring with it increased efficiency, growth and prosperity.

A former colleague of mine, Professor Peter Bauer, has written eloquently on this issue, and I cannot resist quoting from his provocative article on 'The investment fetish'. Writing of the situation in Third World countries today, he states that

> Emergence from poverty . . . does not require large scale capital formation. It requires changes in attitudes and mores adverse to

material improvement, readiness to produce for the market instead of subsistence and the pursuit of appropriate government economic policies. Much of capital formation is not a pre-condition of material advance but its concomitant.[14]

The second proposition is that wealth has been created more effectively within a market economy rather than a state-owned or planned economy.

This is true historically and it is true of the world today. The Industrial Revolution took place in a world characterised by widespread private property rights and free markets. That had not always been so in England. The medieval economy was based on communal property rights and large monopolies. But before the 'take-off' occurred in Great Britain, new institutional arrangements had come into being which guaranteed that reward was related to effort. The enclosure movement secured private property rights over land. The establishment of joint-stock companies and corporations enabled firms to retain profits based on large-scale production. Patent laws meant that those responsible for inventions and innovations could realise a positive rate of return on their investments.

Not only did the law guarantee that those who saved, invested and innovated were rewarded, but people had confidence in the stability and objectivity of the legal system and, most of all, in the fact that it could not easily be manipulated and tampered with by the Crown or the government. A capitalist economy depends for its success on entrepreneurs taking risks. The one guarantee which entrepreneurs need is a strong legal system which ensures that they reap the advantages from successful risk-taking. By the late eighteenth century the British economy offered entrepreneurs great certainty as far as the legal and political systems were concerned. As a result, they were free to calculate the commercial risks attached to different activities, and make their decisions accordingly. The result of this business climate was a remarkable increase in productivity associated with the coming of industrialisation.

It is precisely this system of property rights which is denied in socialist countries. Rewards are not related to effort and commercial risk-taking, but to party membership, bureaucratic status, political fiat and corruption. As a consequence, the legitimate commercial entrepreneurial spirit is killed; for perfectly understandable reasons, people devote their resources to hacking a way through the political and bureaucratic jungle of their economies. It would be a great surprise therefore if the productivity of capital and labour were anything like as great under this system, as it is under capitalism.

We must, however, let the facts speak for themselves. After sixty-five years of socialism, the Soviet Union remains a remarkably inefficient economy. It is widely reported that private agricultural land, which is about 3 per cent of total arable land, accounts for between a quarter and a third of the country's total agricultural output.[15] Authorities on the Soviet economy have estimated that the real wages of Soviet industrial workers were not much greater in 1970 than in 1913. The real income of Soviet agricultural workers has been estimated as just about 1.2 per cent higher in 1969 than it was in 1913.[16] In the mid-1970s, living space per person in the USSR was eleven square metres, which was about one half of that of Western Europe during this period.[17] These dismal statistics accord with the more impressionistic press reports of continuing shortages, queues, rationing and lack of foreign exchange for the average Soviet citizen.

The evidence is not confined to the Soviet Union. The contrast between the creation of wealth in market and non-market economies can also be seen in the economic performances of East and West Germany, India and Japan, and most of all, those Third World countries committed to substantial state involvement in economic life and those committed to the value of the market. Table 1 contrasts the differing fortunes in terms of GNP growth per capita over the 1970s of various countries committed to different kinds of economic systems.

TABLE 1. *GNP* per capita growth rates 1970–79 in Third World economies

Market-oriented		State-planned	
South Korea	10.3%	Ghana	−0.1%
Taiwan	9.9%	India	1.4%
Hong Kong	9.4%	Liberia	1.8%
Singapore	8.4%	Nepal	2.7%
Ivory Coast	6.7%	Bangladesh	3.3%
Kenya	6.5%	Sri Lanka	3.8%
Malawi	6.3%	Burma	4.3%

Sources: The World Bank, *Accelerated development in Sub-Saharan Africa: an agenda for action*, Washington DC, 1981, p. 36.
The World Bank, *The World Development Report 1982*, Washington DC, 1982.
John C. H. Fei, Gustav Ranis, S. W. Y. Kuo, *Growth with equity: the Taiwan case*, Oxford University Press, 1979, p. 36.

The third proposition is that the take-off to sustained economic growth in the Western world took place within the context of a Christian civilisation.

Industrialisation and sustained economic growth did not originate in societies dominated by Animism, Hinduism or Shintoism. This is not to argue necessarily that there is a simple causal connection between Christian values and industrialisation but merely to observe a fact of history.

Too often we forget how unique the widespread wealth of the Western world is when judged by historical norms. For most of human history, poverty and recurring famine have been the lot of mankind. This is not to underestimate the achievements of ancient civilisations. In ancient India technology and organisation were both developed and their achievements in constructing dams, roads, temples and public buildings were very great. In ancient Chinese society, a number of quite fundamental inventions took place – gunpowder, the magnetic compass, printing. As the Greek Empire expanded the Mediterranean became a great trading area, which was eventually extended to the Near and Middle East. Tertullian, one of the Church Fathers, writing at the beginning of the third century of the achievement of Rome, could say that:

> The World is every day better known, better cultivated and more civilised than ever before. Everywhere roads have been built, the countryside explored and every part of it opened to commerce. Smiling fields have abolished the forest; flocks and herds have routed the wild beasts; the sands have been sown; the rocks broken up and cleared, the marshes drained. There are now as many towns and cities as once there were cottages. Reefs and shoals have lost their terrors. Wherever there is a trace of life, there are houses, buildings and well-ordered government.[18]

But industrialisation as we know it today is a feature of the modern world. The Industrial Revolution started in the late eighteenth century in England, then spread through the countries of Western Europe – Holland, France, Germany – and then in the nineteenth century spread to North America and to the various colonies of the British Empire. The results of industrialisation have been different qualitatively from anything experienced previously. In the nineteenth century the population of Great Britain increased four-fold. But despite this real wages *doubled* between 1800 and 1850 and *doubled* again between 1850 and 1900. The production and consumption of wage-goods increased by something like 1600 per cent throughout the nineteenth century. The same was true of other countries. Before the Industrial Revolution the growth rate of leading European countries was at most 1 per cent a year, in many cases nil and some cases negative. But between 1870 and 1914 the growth rate of the twelve leading industrial countries averaged 2.7 per cent. For the US over this period, growth averaged no less than 4.3 per cent per year.[19]

Many different theories have been put forward for the ultimate stagnation of ancient economies and the sustained growth of the European economies of the nineteenth century. Unless one is a Marxist historian, and therefore rejects out of hand the role which values play in changing the economic circumstances of society, nearly all of the other explanations have, directly or indirectly, to do with the importance of values. For example, W. W. Rostow in *How It All Began* concludes that:

> . . . the critical failure of the traditional societies was conceptual: science – lively and irresistible as it was – did not teach those with access or power over resources that the physical world could be understood in ways that permitted it systematically to be transformed to their advantage. More passive and fatalistic views of man's relation to the physical world, therefore prevailed.[20]

The most explicit thesis regarding the effect of culture in shaping the values needed for modern economic life is that developed by Weber. He observed that the impulse to acquisition and associated activities – such as trading, money-lending and the setting up of capitalistic enterprises – had been a feature, to a greater or lesser degree, of almost all known civilisations, including medieval Europe. Nevertheless there is a distinction between this kind of capitalism and modern capitalism: the latter involves the systematic organisation of economic life for the pursuit of profit by means of continuous, rational capitalistic enterprise in the context of a free labour market. Weber was particularly impressed with what he called the spirit (*geist*) of capitalism which infused this new approach. For this to be possible, traditional (medieval) values needed to be overturned and replaced by a creed or social philosophy which gave a specific legitimacy to private property, profit and wealth creation. According to Weber this is precisely what the Reformation and the theology of Calvin, Luther, Baxter and the Puritans supplied. Work was a 'calling', so that the creation of wealth acquired a sanctity. Diligence, thrift, sobriety, prudence – the moral qualities which the Reformation emphasised – were precisely those qualities which turned out to be crucial to successful commercial life. The direct consequences of this world-view for the process of wealth creation arose from the Puritan concern to place an upper limit on personal consumption. The Puritans rejected the extravagance and ostentation of feudal society, and opted for a more simple middle-class standard of life. The implications were very carefully noted by Weber.

> When the limitation of consumption is combined with this release of acquisitive society, the inevitable practical result is obvious; accumulation of capital through ascetic compulsion to save. The restraints which were imposed upon the consumption of wealth naturally served to increase it by making possible the productive investment of capital.[21]

As Weber was the first to acknowledge, it is not easy to demonstrate this thesis empirically. He himself cites as evidence the Puritan business classes in North America and Holland, who were concerned with the rational capitalistic organisation of private property and free labour and who were motivated by the desire to perform the duties of their God-given vocation.[22] More recently, the lifestyles and business successes of English non-conformists have been seen to confirm the validity of Weber's argument about the economic outlook and everyday conduct of ascetic Protestants.

> Successful mediaeval business men died with feelings of guilt and left money to the Church to be put to unproductive uses. Successful protestant business men were no longer ashamed of their productive activities whilst alive, and at death left money to help others to imitate them . . .[23]

For myself, two things are particularly important about this general thesis. The first is that I find it very hard to understand the development of capitalism and industrial society in the West without taking into account those distinct cultural and religious values which shaped the ethos of personal responsibility, honesty, thrift, diligence and rational calculation, values which upheld private property rights, and which provided a distinct perspective on work and profits.[24] One can think of many other cultures and value systems which have been inimical to capital accumulation and industrialisation precisely because they give little place to such values.[25]

The second is that the Protestant ethic thesis turns out to be a specific example of a far more general thesis: namely, that the economic process is related in an important way to cultural and religious values.[26] If this is true it has profound implications not only for the present problems of the Third World but also for those of the West itself.

Factors Conducive to Wealth Creation

As we study the historical process of wealth creation and observe the performances of modern economies, it becomes clear that some factors are conducive, and by implication, some factors are a hindrance, to wealth creation. Let us consider each in turn.

First, there is the matter of *ownership*. We have seen that market economies are more efficient than state-owned economies in creating wealth. We can also see from the experience of European countries how inefficient public-sector enterprises tend to be. In all countries, there are some public-sector enterprises which are successfully managed and which yield a profit or surplus. But the British experience suggests that they are not representative. Public corporations in the United Kingdom (coal, gas, electricity, BNOC, airways, railways) made aggregate losses between 1970 and 1980 of no less than £4.2 billion. Over the same period they paid £41.1 billion to purchase fixed capital assets, which they financed along with their trading losses by subsidies of £10.5 billion, capital transfer from government of £2.8 billion and write-offs of debt to government of £1.8 billion. The root cause of the problem of public-sector enterprises is high wages and overmanning, which means high unit cost and low productivity. For example, in 1978, British Airways (which on a typical day employs more staff than it flies fare-paying passengers) averaged 410 million passenger miles per staff member each year, while US airlines averaged 546 million. In 1980 the British coal industry produced 550 tons per head; the West German coal industry 1000 tons per head, and the American coal industry 3500 tons per head. In 1980 British Leyland (which is in reality a public enterprise) produced three and a half cars per man year: Toyota produced no less than seventy-two![27]

The British experience suggests that one major reason publicly-owned companies perform so poorly is that they are vulnerable to political pressures – their pricing and investment programmes are trimmed for political not commercial reasons. Another is that they are open to being taken over by trade unions – which leads inevitably to high wages and overmanning, so that they lack the commercial flexibility of the private sector to shed excess labour once they start making losses. In other words, public ownership results in the politicisation of the enterprise, which in turn leads to poor commercial performance.

Ownership cannot easily be separated from incentive. The reason that private ownership encourages efficiency and growth is that the rewards from hard work, innovation, risk-taking, restructuring and investment accrue to those who take the decisions. This is most evident in small businesses and partnerships, somewhat less true in large private-sector organisations and least of all in public-sector organisations. It is impossible to create similar incentives in nationalised industries to those which exist for businessmen with equity interest in small firms. Hence it is wrong to separate ownership from incentives.

Next, there is the question of *markets*. A government can take one of two views of markets. Either it can foster the market economy by allowing markets the necessary freedom to do their work, or else it can attempt to control markets by controlling prices, restricting supply and so forth. The choice is really between whether it thinks its own mechanism of planning is superior to that of the market place. Is it in a position to do better than free markets? Many governments in the world clearly feel that they are, which is the reason we have so many non-market economies. As we saw earlier, however, the evidence suggests that markets are far more efficient than governments in allocating resources and the reason has to do with the nature of prices.

Prices perform a variety of functions in a market economy: they supply information about consumer tastes, about the availability of resources and about productive opportunities which helps to coordinate the differing interests of consumers and producers: they provide incentives for people – for workers, entrepreneurs, savers, investors and innovators – to act in a way which most benefits society as a whole: and by determining the levels of wages, rents, interest rates and profits, they distribute income to the working population, equity holders and landowners on the basis of the scarcity value of those resources. The reason a market economy tends to outperform a planned economy is that the ability of the visible hand of planners to transmit information, coordinate economic activity, provide suitable incentives and distribute income is inferior to the 'invisible hand' of the market place.

Third, there is the importance of *political stability*. A businessman expects to have to calculate commercial risks: the possibility that demand may be less than expected, or that wages are greater than expected, or that imported inputs may prove more difficult to obtain, or that interest rates may rise unexpectedly – such are the daily problems of running a business. But the extent to which a businessman can assume political risk is limited: the possibility that his assets may be expropriated, or that compensation is less than adequate, or that exchange controls are imposed which restrict the ability to repatriate profits, or that labour cannot be freely chosen and employed, are problems with which it becomes very difficult to deal and to remain in business. The threat of political instability and the likelihood of these kinds of risks is therefore a major problem for any company contemplating doing business in a particular country especially if it is committing funds in the form of an investment.

Last, there is the question of *culture*. The contemporary accepted wisdom on this matter is that cultural differences play a minor role in explaining differential rates of economic growth between countries. By its very constitution, the United Nations Organisation and its agencies are required to maintain a strict neutrality as far as culture – and its influence on economic development – is concerned. Although not an official report of the United Nations, the prevailing view was made quite explicit by Herr Brandt in his introduction to the Brandt Report: 'We take it for granted that all cultures deserve equal respect, protection and promotion.'[28]

This is a view which Max Weber could well have held at a personal level; but on the basis of his own research, it would hardly have constituted the kind of recommendation that he might have made to a Third World government concerned with fostering economic growth. The one feature of modern capitalism which Weber emphasised was its appeal to rationality. Unlike other economic systems, it was not based on custom and tradition, but on deliberate calculation relating to efficiency, least cost, improved profit, changing demand, new marketing and purchasing techniques, increased rigour of work supervision. According to Weber, this kind of rationality fitted in with a Reformation world view. Biblical Christianity placed emphasis on the world as God's world and the universe as his creation. The image of man which emerged was of a creative, evaluative, resourceful person, with a mandate to transform his environment in response to his earthly calling.

But this view fits in uneasily with many contemporary religions. Many world religions have a decidedly fatalistic element. In a recent book, *The Third World Calamity*, Brian May examines the cases of Islam, Hinduism and animism.[29] He quotes Niels Mulder, the Dutch anthropologist, who says of the Javanese, who are Muslim: 'The strong emphasis on the nonentity of the individual, the values of *negli* (giving way, flowing with the stream) of *narima* (acceptance), *sabar* (patience), and the idea of cosmic inevitability – all of these give strong support to the wisdom of passive endurance in the hope of better times to come.'[30] A very similar fatalism can be found in the Shi'ite approach in Islam in which each believer must accept the religious authority of an ayatollah, which is binding over not only the sacred but also the secular aspects of life. Rodinson in his book on *Islam and Capitalism* suggests one reason why there might be some basis for the observation that Muslim cultures tend to encourage a passive approach to economic life:

> In reality Muhammed was reacting in his own way against the fatalism of pre-Islamic ideology, the view current among the Arabs, of the dominance of blind laws of fate imposed upon men as upon the gods, a prefiguring of the determinism of the idea of natural laws. He replaced the omnipotence of fate by that of personal will, the will of Allah, whom one could at least invoke, pray to and supplicate.[31]

Such a culture, so May argues, is a constraint on Iranian development. Iranian culture has been taken up with poetry, philosophy, the arts and dreams of the past and the future.[32] At heart it is an anti-rationalistic culture. By contrast, a Western-type economic system requires a rationalistic culture of the kind emphasised by Weber.

Another example of this general thesis has to do with the concept of time. The accumulation of capital and successful economic development require that the entrepreneur think over a long time-horizon. Yet the animistic concept of time – which, mixed up with Buddhism, pervades Thailand for example – would rule this out.

> In an Animistic world view the small and continuous communal group knows itself to be surrounded by a vast amount of diffuse, amoral power with which it makes short-term contracts to ensure safety and protection . . . This Animistic perception of

> short-term order in a sea of uncertainty seems to be the most pregnant of Thai time perspectives.[33]

It is not difficult to understand, once again, why such a culture as this may be inimical to economic development. Yet it is in marked contrast to the Judaeo–Christian world-view. As a religion Christianity affirms a beginning, a present and an ending to the human drama. Time was inaugurated by God; it is in time that God has progressively revealed himself: and the Christian looks forward to a day when time will be no more. Meanwhile the mandate to Christians is 'Occupy till I come', with an emphasis on the need to be prepared and to be diligent in view of a coming judgment.

Rationalistic Humanism and the Crisis of Wealth Creation

The issue of culture is not something which is only relevant to the emergence of capitalism in the Western world, or in contrasting certain First and Third World societies. It is also relevant to the Western crisis itself. The dominant philosophy of the Western world at present is a secular humanism. It forms the direct legacy of the Renaissance and the Enlightenment. It worships freedom and makes a virtue of science and yet it is at heart anti-rational, nihilistic and materialist.

It was analysed most clearly by Solzhenitsyn in his famous Commencement Address at Harvard University in June 1978.

> . . . rationalistic humanism . . .: the proclaimed and practised autonomy of man from any higher force above him. It could also be called anthropocentricity, with man seen as the centre of all . . . The humanistic way of thinking which has proclaimed itself our guide, did not admit the existence of intrinsic evil in man, nor did it see any task higher than the attainment of happiness on earth. It started modern Western civilization on the danger-

ous trend of man worshipping his material needs. Everything beyond physical well-being and the accumulation of material goods, all other human requirements and characteristics of a subtler and higher nature, were left outside the area of attention of state and social systems, as if human life did not have any higher meaning. These gaps were left open for evil, and its draughts blow freely today.[34]

In considering the present crisis of Western economies, modern economics has a bias against attributing importance to cultural and religious values. The major emphasis is invariably placed on differing economic systems with their differing systems of property rights, incentives and market structures. As a result, the typical experiment which Milton Friedman, for example, performs is the following. Take two societies which are similar in most respects, except in their system of economic organisation: East and West Germany, North and South Korea, Hong Kong and mainland China, Japan and India. Then consider the contrast in economic performance. It turns out to be quite remarkable. It seems not unreasonable to argue therefore that the major factor responsible for such differences is the system of economic organisation. In all the above examples the conclusion drawn is that the market economy unambiguously outperforms the non-market economy. I am convinced that such an experiment is valid and important and that the evidence shows conclusively that in terms of wealth creation free markets are far more efficient than regulated economies.

But I believe there is another experiment which needs to be performed, which may prove to be of even greater importance for the future of the Western world. Take two societies which are similar in most respects except their cultural and religious values; and then examine the implications of these specific kinds of differences. To do this we can compare different societies at a point in time, or we can examine the same society at different points in time. The most distinctive feature of the West over recent years is the way in which its '*geist*' has changed since the time it was examined by Weber.

Puritanism was complementary to a rational economic system, because its world-view was grounded in the concept of a created order which had a purpose and a destiny, and which worked according to rules. The outstanding feature of contemporary Western culture is its thoroughly secularised and humanistic basis. If the contemporary philosophy of the West is anti-rational, nihilistic and purposeless, does it have any implications for economic life?

I believe it does, and that it is certainly possible at an analytical level to contrast two kinds of capitalist economy – one centred on faith and God, the characteristics of which Weber analysed so carefully, and the other centred on hedonism and Mammon and standing in contrast to Reformation thought. One type of economy has a view of work as a calling, the other of work simply as a way of getting money; one involves responsibility for the future and hence the need to save and invest, the other is concerned with the present, with the maximising of consumption; one has a strict standard for money and a belief in balanced budgets, the other has abandoned all rules with respect to money creation and government deficits; one views the family as the basic unit in economic welfare, the other the state as the major engine of redistribution; one involves small government, the other large government; one believes in private property, the other state ownership; one involves trade unions remedying injustices, the other involves labour monopolies raising their real income at the expense of fellow workers; one involves corporations concerned with more than profit in a world of conscious moral choices, the other is involved with economic men, living in an amoral world, maximising profits.

It is too superficial therefore to follow traditional economics and analyse the present crisis of the West exclusively in economic categories: growing government, oil-price shocks, rapid money-supply growth. The crucial questions are why these have taken place and I believe they can only be answered outside of the prison of conventional economics. If culture matters for economic life, and a strong case can be made for the fact that it does, then it is inconceivable that the changing mores of Western civilisation over the past few decades have left economic life unchanged.

3

THE THEOLOGICAL DIMENSION

In a world in which there is so much poverty, hunger and disease, the very fact that market economies are capable of creating wealth more effectively than socialist economies seems in itself a good enough reason to advocate the extension of the free-enterprise economy. But for the Christian who wishes to defend the market economy, there is one very real problem. If we take the text of the gospels seriously, it seems at first sight as if there is a grave inconsistency between the teachings of Jesus on the subject of wealth and poverty and the principles on which market economies depend for their success.

In the West today we tend to judge economic success in terms of prosperity: a rapid rate of economic growth, rising per capita consumption, a continual accumulation of wealth. Yet when Jesus addressed the prosperous people of his day, it was not to congratulate them but to warn them. 'How hard it is for those who have riches to enter the Kingdom of God',[1] 'Do not lay up for yourselves treasures on earth',[2] 'Blessed are you poor',[3] 'Woe to you that are rich',[4] 'A man's life does not consist in the abundance of his possessions',[5] 'You cannot serve God and mammon',[6] 'It is easier for a camel to go through the eye of a needle than for a rich man to enter the kingdom of God'.[7] We applaud the market economy because it enables people to prosper. Yet prosperity was the very thing which Jesus warned against in his teaching.

Then there is the matter of property. The market economy depends for its success on private property, because private ownership enables people to reap for themselves the benefits of hard work and shrewd investment. A socialist economy does not enable people to do this, and for that reason socialism is not nearly as successful as capitalism. But certain of the sayings of Jesus on property fit in uneasily with such a position. 'Sell all that you have and distribute to the poor . . . and come, follow me;'[8] '. . . they left everything and followed him,'[9] 'Give to every one who begs from you; and of him who takes away your goods do not ask them again,'[10] 'whoever of you does not renounce all that he has cannot be my disciple.'[11] The early Church took this teaching literally. The Church in Jerusalem shared their material possessions. When the occasion demanded those with property sold it, so that there were no needy people in the community of the Jerusalem Church. When subsequently as a Church they became poor, St Paul appealed to other Churches to help them. The principle which he advanced was that of equality and the basis of his argument was the Incarnation: 'For you know the grace of our Lord Jesus Christ, that though he was rich, yet for your sake he became poor, so that by his poverty you might become rich.'[12]

Yet another possible area of conflict is the contrast between the competitive and individualistic ideals of the market economy and the sense of community and caring which is emphasised in the New Testament. The most well-known metaphor which is used to describe the Church in the epistles is that of the body of Christ. The body is a powerful image because it suggests an organic unity which exists within the Church and which cuts across all known barriers of race, nationality, status, wealth or power. Its practical impact derives from the fact that within the body relationships are not just between the head and an individual member but among individual members themselves. As a result the Christian Church is a trans-national, trans-cultural and trans-racial institution. It would be difficult to find a metaphor which was further removed from Adam Smith's ideal of an atomistic, property-owning, profit-maximising society than that of the body.

Whatever one's preconceived views, the teaching of Christ and the practice of the early Church cannot be dismissed lightly. There is no doubt that for many, over the centuries, it has formed the basis for a certain kind of socialism. A society in which the individual has a responsibility to the community, and in turn, in which the community has a responsibility to the individual, is seen as the ideal of Christian economic life. In England this was the view of Christian socialism in the nineteenth century. More recently it has been put within a Third World perspective. In his lifestyle and teaching it is claimed that Jesus identified himself with the poor. A recent book by a Dutch theologian on the subject claims that 'The gospel is written from the perspective of the poor man' and Jesus is seen as the embodiment of the poor person.[13] He was born in a stable, owned nothing throughout his life, and died in poverty. If at the same time it is assumed that poverty and wealth are not independent phenomena but that the poverty of some is the direct consequence of the wealth of others, then the resulting economic inequality is viewed as the consequence of the structures of society. Jesus was therefore seen as a member of the exploited proletariat, suffering because of unjust economic structures but nevertheless graciously identifying with others of his class. It was because of his suffering and his strong sense of justice that at the beginning of his ministry Jesus proclaimed that the poor were to hear the good news, the captives were to be released and the oppressed were to be liberated. His life and ministry were directed to this end. If the process he inaugurated is to be continued, so contemporary theologians argue, it means the radical transformation of those structures which create inequality. The Christian is involved therefore in a fight against private property, money, profit, competition and everything else associated with the market economy. It is an opposition which should not just be marginal but total.

What did Jesus Really Teach?

Until we come to terms with what Jesus really taught on the subject of wealth and poverty we shall never face up to the full weight of the theological objections to the market place. If Jesus's teaching simply amounted to a straightforward attack on wealth and an identification with the cause of the poor, as the above thesis suggests, it would at least be relatively easy to understand. But in terms of what Jesus actually said and did, matters are not that simple.

There is another side to Jesus's teaching on all these issues. The parables of the talents, the pounds and the unjust steward were all spoken to the disciples.[14] They were all concerned with the proper management of resources and the lesson of each is that the Christian has a responsibility to use his resources in the best interests of the Kingdom of God. Private ownership is never defended but taken for granted in these parables, and the resourcefulness of those who increased their wealth applauded. In addition, Jesus upheld the Mosaic law which commanded children to support their parents and encouraged people to give charitably;[15] but financial support and charitable giving require the resources to be able to do so. In his lifestyle, Jesus accepted dinner invitations from the rich, used for himself resources provided by his friends and never suggested that as a rule for living his followers (such as Zacchaeus) were to sell all they possessed.[16] For all who sought the Kingdom of God the promise was that 'all these things [material needs] shall be added unto you'.[17]

The temptation facing each one of us is to interpret Jesus's teaching to fit our preconceived ideas on these matters or else simply to justify our present lifestyle and interests. I believe that it is all too easy to argue that the parable of the talents justifies private ownership, private profit and inequality, and yet ignore his warnings to the wealthy. But it is just as easy to listen to his indictment of the prosperous and ignore his teaching on property and stewardship. The fact that Jesus is variously portrayed as social reformer, revolutionary socialist and compassionate capitalist suggests that the task of interpretation is not easy. It is easy to be selective: but it is difficult to hold together the seemingly diverse strands of his teaching.

On reflection, however, it becomes clear that there is within the life and teaching of Jesus a basic unity which is centred around what he called the Kingdom of God. For the Jewish society into which he was born, Jesus was seen in messianic terms. Despite poverty around him and the oppression and injustice of the colonial situation in which he found himself, he rejected a secular interpretation of salvation. When tempted, he refused to turn stones into bread. In a similar vein he refused to establish a government which would throw off the shackles of Roman domination. His primary task was to establish a kingdom but it was a kingdom whose dimensions were spiritual and not secular. Whenever and wherever anyone accepted the authority of God over their life, there and then the Kingdom of God was extended. The Kingdom meant the reign of God over the lives of individuals. As a result it was impossible for mortals to build this Kingdom. It was established by God; and its extension depended on the Holy Spirit. 'The Kingdom, as Jesus knew it was God's, and men could no more establish it than they could make the sun rise in heaven . . . His attitude was always that of waiting on God, of trust in a divine power and wisdom that working on our behalf will accomplish for us what we cannot do ourselves.'[18]

The essence of the Kingdom was that it viewed man's fundamental problem as spiritual and not political; it was established in response to the deepest and most intractable of human problems, namely man's independence of God. Jesus was no legislator or political activist by today's standards and the Kingdom was not set up by campaigning for greater justice in the Roman administration or joining the guerilla movement for national independence. Even if Jesus had been handed political power and offered the position of procurator or even Emperor, it would have been an irrelevance to his basic purpose. It would have been then, and remains to this day, impossible to legislate the things about which he talked and preached, simply because the ethic of his Kingdom was love and the source of its power supernatural.

When the Kingdom is viewed in these terms Jesus's teaching acquires a distinct emphasis. Take for example the inaugural address in Luke's gospel, when the Messiah announces that he is the fulfilment of Isaiah's prophecy and outlines his ministry with these words: 'The Spirit of the Lord is upon me, because he has anointed me to preach good news to the poor. He has sent me to proclaim release to the captives and recovering of sight to the blind, to set at liberty those who are oppressed, to proclaim the acceptable year of the Lord.'[19] This passage is frequently interpreted to lend support to the establishment of a welfare state, revolutionary change, or the campaign for human rights. Whatever the merits of demands for these things may be I find it impossible to believe that these words should be understood in political terms. They are best understood in terms of what Jesus actually did during the three-year period of his ministry which directly followed his making them. He went about and did preach the good news to the poor, he miraculously healed the blind, he liberated those who had been imprisoned by evil spirits, he healed a great many people. There is no evidence whatever to suggest that his own interpretation of these words, judged by what he actually did during his own ministry, involved a call to political action.

All of this is very important as a background to Jesus's teaching on wealth. In this teaching Jesus was concerned with enunciating principles, not policies. He was not concerned directly with the creation of wealth or the removal of poverty. He did not examine in any detail the causes of either wealth or poverty or any connection which there might be between them. He did not explore at all the relationships which might have existed between the inequality of wealth and poverty in his own day and the structures of his own society. How much surplus was extracted from Palestine by Rome? Were the rural poor the result of urban affluence? Was all wealth the result of exploitation? Should land be communally owned? Yet these are the questions which contemporary theologians and churchmen would have had him ask. But he did not, and it is significant that he did not. As we say earlier, because of the nature of the Kingdom he had come to establish, it is inconceivable that he would have concerned himself with issues such as these.

Yet in his parables and encounters with people he frequently talked of money; once again not in the context of some programme for economic reform but in terms of personal spiritual destiny. And it is in this context that a number of clear principles emerge from his teaching. The first is that there is nothing intrinsically wrong with wealth or particularly virtuous about poverty. The ownership of goods, houses and clothes is not a sin. Jesus had friends who owned such things and he himself stayed in their homes and went in their boats. In the various parables which deal with profit and investment such as those of the talents or the pounds, or those which deal with wages and employment, such as that of the steward, there is never a suggestion that work, business, banking or investment were of themselves wrong. In the parable of the rich fool, the fool is not criticised because his business was profitable or because of his desire to expand his capital assets: he was criticised because his life was centred on his own ego and because in consequence he was totally unconcerned about God.[20]

There are, however, two passages which might seem to contradict this principle. One is the story of Dives and Lazarus.[21] It might seem from this as if wealth or poverty is sufficient in itself to determine an individual's destiny. As is clear from the later part of the story, however, the rich man throughout his life, like the foolish farmer mentioned earlier, had lived a totally self-centred and godless life. His use of wealth and his neglect of Lazarus's needs were evidence of this fact. By contrast the implication to be drawn, even though it is not made explicit in the text is that Lazarus was a man of faith. The reason for this is that Dives, in pleading on behalf of his brothers, accepted the need for repentance as a condition for the position in which Lazarus found himself.

To suggest that Lazarus was finally received by God simply because he was poor would be in violation of everything which Jesus ever taught about sin, repentance, new birth, redemption and entry into his Kingdom.

The other passage is Luke's record of the first of the beatitudes, 'Blessed are you poor, for yours is the kingdom of God', which suggests that poverty is itself a virtue. The expression refers to those who are literally poor. The Greek word used means 'one who is so poor as to have to beg', that is the physically destitute. This passage might refer to those early Christians who became Christians from a background of real poverty. They experienced what it meant to become part of the Kingdom of God, and in a literal sense they were blessed. More likely, however, is that it refers to a poverty of spirit. It is quite common in the Old Testament to read of poverty as a shorthand for poverty of spirit. True poverty was humility before God. In this sense the passage means that the benefits of the Kingdom will only be received by those who come to God from a sense of need. Also significant is the fact that Matthew's account of the beatitudes reads 'Blessed are the poor in spirit, for theirs is the kingdom of heaven', so that no possible ambiguity arises over its meaning. Once again, to suggest that only those who are poor in an economic sense will inherit the Kingdom is artificially to isolate Luke's gospel and make a nonsense of most of the rest of Jesus's teaching.[22]

A second principle which may be drawn from the gospels is our responsibility for the use of our resources. We are trustees of what God has given us and the Bible makes it perfectly clear that he has given us everything we possess. For example, in the Sermon on the Mount Jesus assumes that all his disciples will give charitably and his major concern is that it should be done in an unostentatious manner. The parable of the talents is frequently used to show Jesus's concern for proper stewardship. The primary intention of the parable of the talents, however, is not the stewardship of financial wealth but of spiritual wealth; it was meant as a warning to the religious leaders of Israel who had been endowed in a very special way with God's revelation. Nevertheless, it is difficult not to broaden the lesson of the parable so that its meaning extends to all the resources which we have been given. Similarly, in the parable of the unjust steward, the steward is commended for acting astutely and Jesus follows the parable by urging his disciples to use what he terms the 'mammon of unrighteous' in just as astute a manner in order to further the interests of his own Kingdom. Then he draws a parallel between the trusteeship of earthly wealth and the wealth of the Kingdom of God and reflects: 'If then you have not been faithful in the unrighteous mammon, who will entrust to you the true riches?'[23] Again in the poetic description of the final judgment in terms of sheep and goats, those who are favoured are commended for feeding the hungry, giving drink to the thirsty, entertaining strangers in their homes, clothing the naked, visiting those who were sick and in prison: the implication of this being that those who are members of the Kingdom have a responsibility to live by its laws.[24]

A third principle which emerges from Jesus's teaching concerns the spiritual hazards which attach to wealth. The mere fact of owning wealth tends to produce a spirit of arrogance and self-reliance. Success tends to breed a philosophy of possessiveness: things become mine, my money, my property, my company, my workforce. Wealth gives people a false sense of security: it deadens the life of the spirit; it makes people unresponsive to the good news of the gospel. According to Jesus it leads to an indifference to the suffering and poverty of the world. In the story of Dives and Lazarus, Dives lived in extravagance; even though Lazarus would have enjoyed the scraps from his feasts, Dives himself was either totally unaware of Lazarus's needs or else totally unresponsive to them. It is impossible to serve God and Mammon: God demands from his followers a spirit of self-denial and sacrifice; Mammon encourages a spirit of self-indulgence and pride.

The Background to Jesus's Teaching

In trying to come to terms with Jesus's teaching on economic matters, it is important that they are set in the context of the Hebrew world of which he was part. Jesus was born in Palestine, a Jew; he was circumcised at birth and educated in the synagogue; from his own words we discover that he thought of the Old Testament as inspired and authoritative and the law as a divinely given rule of life, which has an enduring validity. In view of this we should not expect to find in Jesus's teaching an exhaustive treatment of those matters which are dealt with at length in the Old Testament, as this was something he assumed those whom he taught would know. In view of this it is important that we consider the teaching of the Old Testament on matters relating to wealth.

The Material World

The very first words of the Book of Genesis lay the foundation for Hebrew thought, 'In the beginning God created the heaven and the earth'. The material world of which we are part is a created order and Yahweh is its creator. He is not a part of his creation; he is not to be equated with trees and flowers and rocks; he is separate. But although separate from his creation, the universe is not like some grand machine which once set in motion runs on for ever. God is outside of his creation, but it still depends on his active involvement for its continuation and survival. Yahweh is a God who cares for his creation. In the New Testament it becomes clear that the one who sustains the world is none other than the Incarnate Christ.[25] In the Epistle to the Hebrews we read that God 'has spoken to us by a Son, whom he appointed the heir of all things, through whom also he created the world. He reflects the glory of God and bears the very stamp of his nature, upholding the universe by his word of power.'[26] This is very different from secular thought. The Hebrew world is quite different from the world of Aristotle or the world of the Enlightenment. For Aristotle the world is intricate and structured but above all rational. For the Enlightenment the world is like some complex machine created by a benevolent God. But in neither is there a God who cares about his creation and who is involved continuously in its wellbeing.

Another phrase which characterises the early pages of Genesis and the description of creation is 'And God saw that it was good'.[27] It appears no less than six times, being said on each of the days of creation. It is a theme which is taken up frequently in the Psalms.[28] The suggestion is that quite apart from its usefulness to human beings, the created world has a splendour and beauty in itself and as such deserves respect. But this is not the limit of goodness. There is in creation an abundance, a bounty: the promise of a land flowing with milk and honey. Poverty, hunger and famine are not what God intended for this world.

This view of the created world is very different from a great deal of secular philosophy. In Plato's thought there was a strict dualism between the world perceived by the senses – the natural world, always changing and imperfect – and the world perceived by the mind – perfect and fixed, a world of beauty and the source of everything good. It was a short step from this to gnosticism, in which the physical world – and everything having to do with it – was the province of evil. In the Hebrew world there was a unity of the spiritual and the material. This world was God's world, physical and spiritual. Jesus had no trace of platonism or gnosticism in his thinking. God was involved in caring for his creation; the lilies were clothed, the ravens fed and the sparrows watched over. The Christian view of the physical world is important in thinking about the creation of wealth; for the physical world is literally the raw material to which value is added in order that wealth may be created. The two crucial facts about this world are that it is God's and that it is intrinsically good.

But man is part of the created world. Like other animals he too was made from the dust of the earth. 'Dust to dust and ashes to ashes' is true of men and dogs and trees: all are dependent for life on the Creator. But man is also distinct in the whole of creation. We are told that he and he alone is created in the image of God. Uniquely he has the capacity to think and speak, to decide right from wrong, to develop technology and culture; above all to exercise control over the created world. Both man and the animal kingdom receive the commands 'Be fruitful and multiply', but it is only to man that the two special commands to subdue the earth and rule over it are given, and they are closely related to his being created in the image of God.[29]

The Hebrew words for subdue (*kabash*) and rule (*radah*) are strong words. *Kabash* means to stamp on or bring into subjection. *Radah*, which is frequently expressed as dominion, means to trample on as in the treading of grapes or in the expression to prevail against. The choice of these words is important for they leave us in no doubt that man is given authority to control the whole of the created world. The form which this control should take is developed later when God instructs Adam in the garden of Eden 'to till it and keep it'.[30] The emphasis here is not on harnessing and controlling the natural world but on preserving and caring for it. The creation mandate is to be no excuse for an ecological crisis.

The tasks which man is given, and which we have brought together through the words 'subdue', 'rule', 'till', 'keep', are the starting point for a Christian view of work. Man was not created to live in a vacuum; neither was he created for a life of complete leisure, although creation recognises explicitly the need for rest. The fact that man has a desire as well as a need to work results from his being created in the image of God. It is no accident that on many occasions the Bible speaks of God as working, as for example in the six days of creation. This view of work was one which was shared by Jesus. Before his particular three-year period of ministry he himself worked as a carpenter. Frequently in his teaching he referred to human work: the shepherd, the farmer, the doctor, the sower, the servant, the manager, the fisherman, the labourer. As he faced the cross he referred to the particular 'work' which remained to be done. Similarly, the apostle Paul was a tentmaker and in certain of his letters he makes it very clear that he was proud of the fact that he was financially independent of the local congregation. In writing to the Church at Thessalonica he mentions those who are 'living in idleness',[31] not doing any work and repeats in writing the verbal command which he gave when he visited them: 'If any one will not work, let him not eat'.[32]

It is wrong therefore to think of work as simply being the result of the fall. Nevertheless the fall is important. Again the early pages of Genesis have something to say to us: they teach unequivocally that God passed judgment through the fall in a way which transformed work into toil. All human work – whether physical or mental, skilled or unskilled, creative or routine – takes place in a situation of tension and frustration and involves an element of drudgery regardless of whether it is in an office, a factory, a construction site or the home. But it still remains that it was for work and not for leisure that God created us, for no other reason than that we were thereby to share with him one of his own activities.

The basis of the Christian view of work is the concept of man having been delegated the authority to manage or have dominion over the physical world. This is a privilege because it puts man at the head of the created world. But it also carries a responsibility. Man is in consequence accountable to his Creator for his use of God's resources.

When we put together the Christian views of the physical world and of work, they have major implications for economic life. Man has been created with an urge to control and harness the resources of nature in the interests of the common good, but he is subject to his accountability to God as trustee to preserve and care for it. This process is precisely what an economist would refer to as a responsible form of wealth creation. Anything which transforms the material world so that it can be of greater use to fellow human beings is an act of wealth creation. It may be bringing waste land into cultivation, improving the productivity of existing farmland, extracting minerals and using them in some manufacturing process, or using the products of manufacturing to provide services to other people. In all cases the output at the end of the day is of more value than the sum of the inputs were at the beginning. A businessman concerned with construction, manufacturing, agriculture, extraction or services is involved therefore in the complex task of fulfilling the creation mandate. Of course such a process may be open to abuse: monopoly, corruption, fraud, exploitation and pollution. But we should not judge the legitimacy of the process by its abuse, in the same way that we should not condemn eating because of gluttony, sex because of perversion, worship because of idolatry, or property because of covetousness. At heart the process of wealth creation stems from a fundamental human drive, the result of man being created in the image of God.

Trinity

One of the most mysterious aspects of the Christian faith is the question – Who is God? Yet it turns out that the biblical answer to this question, with its emphasis on Theism rather than Deism and on Trinitarianism rather than Unitarianism, has profound implications for economic life. Already we have noticed in passing that the God whom the Christian worships is a personal God. He has a mind, a will and an existence of his own. He is variously described throughout the Old and New Testaments in terms which we readily understand: he protects, he comforts, he forgives, he warns, he judges, he rescues, he loves. He is not some mysterious supernatural influence or some impersonal Supreme Being. He is God the Father, Christ the Incarnate Son and the living Holy Spirit. As a result, he is very different from the God of Deism. The Deist answer to the question – Who is God? – was in terms of a creator, an architect of the universe, a source of power. The Deist looked to find God in the laws of nature. The God of Deism was essentially an absentee landlord: his power, reason and will were to be found in the universe but he was not a God concerned and involved with his people in a personal way. (As we shall see later, this is critical to understanding the thoughts of Adam Smith.)

The fact that the God of the Christian revelation is a personal God has profound implications for economic life because economic life has a personal dimension as well. The act of employment is not just a legal transaction or some input into a production process; it becomes a personal relationship between two human beings and the work situation becomes a network of such relationships. The act of selling is not just finding a point on a demand curve but a transaction between two people with a God-given sense of absolute standards. The 'market' is not just some construct devised to solve the problem of price determination but a series of individual exchanges between people in which mutual trust is extended and accepted. The profit which is earned on a transaction is paid for and quoted by people with a sense of fairness and equity.

The fact that economic life has this personal dimension has one very important implication. It is impossible for economic life to be personal without it at the same time being moral. If man is created in the image of God then morality is as certain a facet of the personhood of man as it is of God. It is interesting to notice how this method differs from that of economic science. Economics starts with *homo oeconomicus*, economic man or – as some economists have baptised him – rational evaluative, maximising man (REMM). It would be wrong to say that economic man has no personality. He has, but it is the personality of a soulless computer, always searching, always choosing and always groping for a least-cost solution. To all intents and purposes economic man is impersonal. But if we start with an impersonal economic man, we construct an impersonal economic system; and in an impersonal economic system the concerns of the human person become lost. Because morality is part of personality, an impersonal economic system becomes an amoral system as well. Hence the workings of the economic system are held as 'value free', beyond the domain of the moral and immoral, the fair and unfair, and of right and wrong. In fact, for economic man the choice between right and wrong is no different from the choice between two brands of soap powders. The rejection of Theism leads inevitably to a meaningless world.

But the Christian doctrine of the Trinity is more than a belief in a personal God who has revealed himself in a very special way. It is also the mystery of the Three in One, one living and true God. And in the unity of this Godhead there are three persons of one substance, power and eternity – the Father, the Son and the Holy Ghost. Among world religions, the Trinity is unique to Christianity. It affirms that before time there was plurality of persons in the Godhead. God was not alone. He was not some solitary figure, unable to communicate, for whom love was a meaningless idea. The Trinity was a community, a fellowship. The persons of the Trinity related to each other and always have done. This has two important implications. It suggests that the idea of community is crucial to the life of society. Any view of society which analyses behaviour as if the individual were some form of automaton is deficient because it fails to capture the importance of relationships. We were not created to live as Crusoe-like figures. As well as this, there is also the relationship which the Trinity expresses between the one and the many, unity and diversity. In the Trinity the one God does not take precedence over the many persons, neither do the many have priority over the One. When in religion the One is given preference, as in Islam, the consequence has been a form of totalitarian state which attempts to discern the will of Allah. When the many are given priority the result is anarchy. But the tension is one which extends to economic philosophy. Fascism and Marxism are both an attempt to emphasise the one to the exclusion of the many and to find salvation in economic terms through the state. Libertarianism is an attempt to emphasise the many at the expense of the One and is a prescription not just for *laissez faire* but also for anarchy. The relevance of the Trinity is to emphasise both the individual and the state, as well as a large variety of mediating institutions which form the basis of a pluralist society. As far as economic life is concerned these include corporations, partnerships, trade unions, professional associations, committees concerned with setting standards, and so on.

Property

The nature of property rights was a subject dealt with at length in the Mosaic law. The eighth commandment – 'Thou shalt not steal' – guaranteed the right to individual ownership. The penalty for sheep-stealing was multiple restoration and that for stealing a man was death.[33] In addition, there were many laws which dealt with re-allocation of titles to land ranging from the arrangements for the Year of Jubilee to the sabbatical laws and even including restrictions on the use of the capital markets.[34]

The starting point for the Pentateuch on this subject was that all property was owned by God. 'The earth is the LORD's' formed the basis of Hebrew thinking. The Jews were constantly reminded of the fact that it was God who had given them the Promised Land. Ultimate ownership rested with God; nevertheless he delegated dominion over the land to families.[35] As a result private property is the norm for ownership in the Old Testament. The Mosaic law guaranteed the rights of individuals to the ownership of property which included the right to buy and sell.[36] There was never a suggestion that the state or the community should be the owner, because that would in some sense be more just or equitable. In a society which was avowedly theocratic this may seem a little surprising. If there was ever a situation in which one might imagine some form of common ownership – comparable to Nyerere's Ujaama policy in Tanzania – it would have been when the Jews entered the Promised Land. Yet each family received a parcel of land and their rights to it were absolute. This meant that in terms of the Mosaic law they had total and unconditional use of their property. That is the meaning of ownership. This might seem surprising in view of what was said earlier about the ultimate ownership of the land being God's. But it is not in any sense a violation of that fact. The fact that all land was held in trust from God meant that each family had a trusteeship responsibility in the sight of God. They were the stewards of what they owned. That did not undermine the total and absolute rights at law which each family had with respect to their property.

In fact one can go further: unless each family had been given absolute rights of ownership it is difficult to imagine how they would have been able to exercise their trusteeship responsibilities. If the land had been communally owned and its use controlled by, let us say, the priests, this would have made redundant the idea that each family had trusteeship responsibility.

While property rights were absolute, there were nevertheless within Pentateuchal society certain constraints built into the law to prevent ownership falling into the hands of a few large families. Every sabbatical year the land was to lie fallow, its harvest was for the poor and in addition debts were cancelled. Every fiftieth year, the Year of Jubilee, all debts were cancelled and land was to return to its original owners, if ownership had changed.[37] The reason given for this redistribution is that while the people were tenants, the true owner was Yahweh. 'The land is mine and you are but aliens and my tenants.'[38] Usury, the lending of money for interest, was prohibited between fellow Jews.[39] The major purpose of these laws was to put a sharp brake on the ownership of land being concentrated in a small number of families – to prevent a cycle of deprivation developing where those in difficult circumstances sold their land, increased their debt and finally found themselves on a treadmill: a situation little better than slavery. Put more positively, each family had the opportunity of a second chance.

These laws were intended to have far-reaching consequences. If they had been applied it would have been impossible for 'labour' to be in conflict with 'capital'. The problem to which Marx addressed himself arose in a situation where capital was owned by a few, but the majority were without access to that capital, other than by being hired on the labour market. This was precisely the situation which the property laws of the Pentateuch were designed to prevent.

This approach to property was never stated explicitly by Jesus; but it was assumed throughout his teaching. In the parables he told which dealt with property, the right to ownership was not only never questioned, but the lessons which he drew depended on this very fact. The fact that ownership is absolute comes out very clearly in the parable of the labourers in the vineyard.[40] A farmer hires labourers at various times of the day including one at the eleventh hour, telling him that he will pay them a fair wage but without mentioning a specific amount. At the end of the day each is given the same wage. Those who worked longest complained. His reply is significant: 'Take what belongs to you, and go; I choose to give to this last as I give to you. Am I not allowed to do what I choose with what belongs to me? Or do you begrudge me my generosity?' The implication is that ownership involves total discretion. This reaches to the very heart of Jesus's teaching. He was not concerned to coerce individuals into income and wealth redistribution; he respected the freedom which private property implied but wanted to see it used for the interests of others.

The view of property which emerges from the Pentateuch has one very important implication. The freedom and ability to exchange rights to private property constitutes the definition of a free market. A free market is nothing more than an opportunity for property owners to exchange their titles to ownership. Any economic system therefore which involves private property rights also involves to a greater or lesser degree reasonably free markets. From this it follows that markets are likely to be features of all societies, ancient and modern, which allow some degree of economic freedom.

Justice

Another theme which emerges from the Old Testament and which would have formed a background to Jesus's teaching was that of justice. The God of the Old Testament, Yahweh, was a God who executed justice. 'For the Lord your God is God of gods and Lord of lords, the great, the mighty, and the terrible God, who is not partial and takes no bribe. He executes justice for the fatherless and the widow, and loves the sojourner, giving him food and clothing.'[41] The Torah contained many laws which were specifically concerned with justice, quite apart from the Decalogue itself. Some we have already touched on under the subject of property: the laws relating to the Sabbath Year and the Year of Jubilee. If a family had been reduced to poverty and forced to till the land, they could purchase it back at any time and not have to wait till the Year of Jubilee. The gleaning laws were an attempt to ensure that the poor and disadvantaged had access to food. The system of tithes was a form of income tax to support the Jewish priests and effect a redistribution to the poor. Usury was prohibited to prevent the growth of inequality and the phenomenon of permanent deprivation. If loans were made to fellow Jews, collateral could not be demanded. If poverty forced some families into serving others they were not to be treated as slaves but as hired servants. In the Year of Jubilee they were to be set free. If they did become slaves they were to be freed every Sabbath Year with a liberal provision from the slave-owner on their being freed.[42] The laws were meant to be a framework within which economic justice could be established. They were an attempt to ensure that there was never permanent poverty, exploitation or gross inequality within the tribes of Israel.

After the Jews had settled in Canaan around 1200 BC, however, it was not long before problems began to emerge and the historical books record the emergence of serious economic problems. The basic forms of injustice recorded are the exploitation of the disadvantaged, fraud, a corrupt legal system, bribery and dishonesty – many of them linked to violence. It is this which God is against because it is a violation of the Torah and the Torah is the decree of God himself. The most outspoken critics of the injustice which developed, however, were the prophets. The first of these, around 800 BC, was Amos who criticised in no uncertain terms the exploitation of the needy by the wealthy, dishonest trading practices, and the opposition of the rulers to any sense of justice. Isaiah, who came soon after, attacked the accumulation of property – both farmland and houses – by individuals, and also the exploitation of the poor and needy by the wealthy.[43]

Although the prophets exposed the social malaise of their

societies, the attack on injustice is never conducted in purely socio-economic terms. The prophets indict the rich for exploiting the poor. Yet they never suggest that the remedy is therefore an economic redistribution conducted in some sort of spiritual vacuum. They invariably pinpoint the root cause of the trouble as spiritual: the nation has departed from God and economic injustice is one result. The priority therefore is not socio-economic reform but spiritual repentance. In this they showed great insight. Massive redistribution of wealth and complex laws to coerce the rich to divest their properties would be of no avail whatever if there were not a simultaneous commitment on the part of those involved to change their values and behaviour. It was this that the prophets saw as the basis for a just society.

Jesus and the Market Place

Having examined the teaching of Jesus himself and the background to his teaching in the Old Testament, we are now in a better position to deal with the problems raised at the beginning of this chapter, namely the apparent inconsistency between the Christian faith and the market economy.

To start with, there is the legitimacy of economic life itself which is not just an issue for the market economy but for any economic system. We have already noticed our Lord's strictures on the wealthy. In the context of his command to seek first the Kingdom of God and his righteousness, concerns such as responsibility at work, choice in consumption or the value of investment seem trivial if not wicked. In facing this problem we have to start at the beginning, and in the context of Genesis the fundamental affirmation which any Christian must make is that the world in which we live is God's world. He created it and he created us. We bear an integral relationship to the material world and it is because of this that the business of creating and using wealth is a natural activity for mankind. Life itself demands that we be continually involved in the process of wealth creation. The basic necessities for living are not provided like manna; the land has to be cultivated, the sea has to be harvested, minerals have to be extracted, the city has to be supplied with services. God created us with the capacity and the desire to do all these things. Life itself, therefore, demands that we use what God has given us to provide the necessities.

But God intended far more than that. We were not created to live our lives in hunger or on the breadline, in a state of poverty using only the barest minimum. God intended us to enjoy his world. The land which he promised Israel was to be flowing with milk and honey. No Christian should feel a sense of guilt from living in a decent house, driving a solid car, wearing a proper suit of clothes or eating a good meal. If we take seriously the fact that this world is God's world, then the business of creating wealth has a Christian foundation.

But to allow wealth creation legitimacy is not to endow it with autonomy. To allow economic life independence and place no bounds on wealth creation would be to justify a philosophy of materialism. For the world which God created is a spiritual world as well as a material world. God is a spirit, and being created in his image we are possessed of spirit as well. Being made, therefore, from the dust of the earth but endowed with spirit, we are to pursue our lives in a material world, yet in the context of a spiritual order. We have a choice: either we seek God and live by the laws of his Kingdom as Jesus taught in the beatitudes or else we worship money and live for consumption and the creation of a personal fortune. The injunction to seek first the Kingdom of God and his righteousness is to choose the former not the latter. But this is not the same as saying that the life of the spirit is superior to the life of the material world or that the life of the spirit is good while the concerns of the material world are bad. It is rather to expose priorities. The call to seek first the Kingdom of God is not a call to the life of the monastery or to a narrow-minded form of personal piety which rejects the material world. We are to seek God and live by the laws of his Kingdom within the material world which he himself has created and of which we are part. The challenge for the Christian then is not to reject the material world and the creation of wealth in favour of some higher spiritual priority but to serve others through the process of wealth creation in the perspective of serving God.[44]

A second major issue has to do with the relationship between the Kingdom of God as Jesus proclaimed and inaugurated it and the kind of economic system which, it is claimed, follows from it. Numerous writers have argued that the Kingdom of God is far closer to a socialist organisation of economic life than the institutions of a market economy. I believe, however, that this is a view which needs to be challenged. The Kingdom of God which Jesus inaugurated was, as we have seen, a Kingdom whose roots were supernatural, whose nature was spiritual and which for those very reasons was in contrast to the kingdoms of this world. When asked by the Pharisees when his Kingdom would appear, Jesus said, 'The kingdom of God is not coming with signs to be observed', i.e., with spectacular events such as rebellion, revolution or war, 'nor will they say, "Lo, here it is!" or "There!" for behold, the kingdom of God is in the midst of you'.[45] Because the Kingdom of God depends for its very existence on an inward supernatural power, it is impossible to translate it into contemporary social, political and economic institutions. It is made up of new people with new motives and is brought about by the mysterious influence of the Holy Spirit. Even when we take the present manifestation of the Kingdom – namely those who have heard the good news and found for themselves reconciliation and redemption and a new lifestyle in a new community, the Christian Church – we find that the source of its life and the rules by which it lives depend crucially on the presence of the Holy Spirit.

It was because this community was so different from that of a fallen world that St Augustine developed the concept of the two cities – the Civitas Dei and the Civitas Terrara.[46] To attempt to translate the principles of the one in terms of institutions for the other is to court disaster. Even if we were to construct an ideal economic system which followed precisely certain theologians' understanding of the New Testament concept of the Kingdom of God, the attempt to legislate these ideas into practice immediately comes up against the fact that the real world in which we live is a fallen world and not a community of saints. Not only is it impossible to deduce socialism from the Kingdom of God: it is impossible to deduce any economic system. In arguing that a socialist economic system is not the logical outgrowth of the Kingdom, I am not for one moment suggesting that the market economy or democratic capitalism or some such concept follows logically either. The point about the Kingdom is that by design it is God's and not ours.

If we are to have institutions in our society which can cope with the reality of a fallen world then we must look for something much more robust than the spontaneous sharing of the early Church. In terms of social ethics, social structures and economic justice, it is very difficult to derive specific principles from either the gospels or the early Church. To the extent that the Judaeo–Christian religion deals with these matters (and they are never treated exhaustively) such principles are surely to be found in the Pentateuch. The ones which emerge there – private property rather than social ownership, each family having continued access to a permanent stake in economic life, some form of anti-poverty programme – seem more compatible with the modern concept of a social market economy than with some variant of Marxism. There is nothing to suggest in the whole of Scripture that the basic institutions of capitalism are incompatible with a Judaeo–Christian world-view. Quite the opposite. The plurality of institutions and the respect for the human person which underlie Western economic institutions are compatible with a Christian world-view.

4

THE MORAL DIMENSION

So far we have attempted to show that a market economy is more efficient than a non-market economy in producing wealth but that a market economy cannot stand by itself. It requires a certain culture and certain values if it is to have legitimacy. These as well as its basic institutions turn out to be thoroughly compatible with a Judaeo–Christian world-view. Nevertheless, there remain a number of serious criticisms to consider which are based on ethical grounds.

The Profit Motive and Self-Interest

The first criticism we shall consider has to do with the part played by the profit motive and self-interest within a market economy. It is a criticism which can be found in a large variety of writings. In the mid-nineteenth century, writers such as Matthew Arnold, Thomas Carlyle and John Ruskin poured their contempt on the values of industrial capitalism, as did William Morris later in the century.[1] The Victorian literary elite's criticism of the industrial system is well summarised in Robert Blatchford's *Merrie England*: 'The thing is evil. It is evil in its origin, in its progress, in its methods, in its motives and in its effects. No nation can be sound whose motive power is greed.'[2]

Earlier this century, R. H. Tawney in his book *Religion and the Rise of Capitalism* could quote with approval Keynes's opinion that 'modern capitalism is absolutely irreligious, without internal union, without much public spirit, often, though not always, a mere congeries of possessions and persuasion', and then himself go on to give his own view of what makes up capitalism:

> It is that whole system of appetites and values, with its view of the life of snatching to hoard, and hoarding to snatch, which now, in the hour of its triumphs, while the plaudits of the crowd still ring in the ears of the gladiators and the laurels are still unfaded on their brows, seem sometimes to leave a taste as of ashes on the lips of a civilisation which has brought to the conquest of its material environment resources unknown in earlier ages but which has not yet learned to master itself.[3]

Joan Robinson, the well-known Cambridge economist, in a book on economic philosophy, argues that 'if the pursuit of profit is the criterion of proper behaviour there is no way of distinguishing between productive activity and robbery', quoting in her defence an interview with Al Capone in which he stated that: 'This American system of ours, call it Americanism, call it capitalism, call it what you like, gives to each and every one of us a great opportunity if we only seize it with both hands and then make the most of it.'[4]

The steps in this kind of argument run broadly as follows. First, it is alleged that there are two kinds of world: a world of the market place in which there is little or no morality, and a world removed from the market place, a world of the family, of public service, and of the community, which lives and works according to moral principles. Next, it is assumed that in the market place people are dominated by the profit motive, which is a corrupting influence and which produces avarice, greed and selfishness. Indeed it is argued that in a capitalist economy these vices are elevated to the status of virtues. Finally, it is suggested that the market economy pervades the whole of society and therefore destroys, distorts or undermines all relationships other than strictly economic ones. The result is a society which is aggressive, selfish and greedy; in fact precisely the kind condemned by our Lord in the gospels.

The problem with this argument is that each of the three critical steps involves assumptions which are false. To start with there is the basic assumption of the two worlds in which behaviour is fundamentally different. It is frequently thought that because business depends on the pursuit of profit, this reduces those in business to the level of economic man, whereas the public service, the military service, the civil service and professions such as medicine, education, law and the Church require and achieve an attitude of service because they are not constrained by the need to make profit. In business, behaviour is selfish and aggressive while in the home or in the community people are caring and considerate, concerned with the good of others rather than their own narrow self-interest. Such a Jekyll-and-Hyde existence is impossible to justify either logically or empirically. There is no doubt that certain individuals in business are selfish, aggressive and brutish, but it requires more than guilt by association with money to show that this is an inevitable outcome. Similar individuals exist in all walks of life. In principle, there is no reason whatever why people should behave in a dualistic manner. For the person who decides to live by certain moral principles, there need be no difference between behaviour in a market and in a non-market situation. An executive in a business corporation can if he so wishes be just as concerned for his staff as a school teacher might be for pupils, an officer for soldiers, a community worker for the elderly or a vicar for parishioners. Similarly, for the person who wishes to abandon moral principles, this can be done just as well outside of the market place as in it. Selfishness, aggression and rivalry may be just as common in schools, local authorities and even families as in business. The same holds for corporate entities. There are certainly scandals in the business world: bribery, fraud, price fixing, pollution, tax evasion, lying to shareholders. But similar problems exist with governments and trade unions and are not unknown even in voluntary organisations. Moral and immoral behaviour occurs in all human institutions. What determines the morality of behaviour is not the institutions in which decisions are made but the individuals who are taking the decisions.

As far as the second step in the argument is concerned, namely that the profit motive is a corrupting influence, two preliminary points need to be noticed. To the extent that the profit motive as a description of business behaviour is synonymous with the pursuit of economic self-interest, such behaviour is not restricted to the business community. When a consumer buys the week's super-save in the supermarket, she is simply trying to get the best value for money and hold down the costs of the weekly shopping bill. Such a decision is no different in principle from the President of General Motors deciding to locate a new production plant in Korea rather than Belgium because expected costs are lower and profits higher. Similarly a trade unionist who enters into a wage negotiation hoping to get the best deal possible for his members is acting no differently from a corporate executive trying to cut costs in the interests of shareholders. Or consider a widow with a small sum of savings seeking investment advice from a bank manager or a broker: her object is to get the best return on her money. Her objective is no different from a businessman's. In terms of motivation it is impossible to isolate profit and the business community from other parts of our economic system.

Another point which needs to be made is that there is no logical connection between profits and the profit motive. The fact that a business needs to make profits to survive does not imply that the pursuit of profit has to be the single dominant concern of every businessman. One cannot automatically move from an accounting concept to a psychological theory. Like everyone else a businessman must live within his budget, and his ability to earn profits will indicate whether he is able to achieve this. But the businessman is not alone in having to operate within a budget: the same applies to the housewife, the director of a charitable organisation and the headmaster of a school. If they fail they find themselves in debt, which is comparable to a company making losses. No one, however, would suggest that because of the constraint which they face, their behaviour is therefore motivated solely by financial considerations.

Within this context it is easy to misunderstand the expression self-interest. Self-interest is usually taken to be synonymous with selfishness and the incarnation of selfishness is the economist's conception of economic man. But this is to misunderstand self-interest. Self-interest is a characteristic of the highest as well as the lowest kind of human behaviour. A person may act in a self-interested way for a host of reasons, such as the carrying out of responsibilities on behalf of family, friends, colleagues, community or Church. Indeed, as Christians we can go further and argue that self-interest as a characteristic of human behaviour cannot be divorced from that self-respect of which our Lord spoke when he instructed us to love our neighbours as ourselves. What precisely is this self-love which Jesus takes for granted as a feature of human personality? Certainly it is not to indulge and pander to our own ego. Nevertheless, it does imply our having a proper regard for our own welfare. Indeed, unless a person has self-respect in this sense, it is difficult to imagine that he could be of much use to his neighbour. Bernard of Clairvaux saw this clearly many centuries ago in the way he described what he called the four stages of love. At the bottom was 'love of self for self's sake'. Next was 'love of God for self's sake': the use of God and everything which goes with Church attendance and religion to further our own interests. The third stage, 'love of God for God's sake', would seem at first sight misplaced for it seems like the highest form of behaviour. Bernard did not elevate it to the highest stage because he claimed this would result in loss of individuality. For him the highest form of love was 'love of self for God's sake'.[5] The reasoning behind this position is that if we take the Bible seriously when it says that God loves each one of us, then we should be able to love ourselves. It is nothing less than an insult to the Almighty if we consider ourselves worthless and wretched when he views us differently. This is not to deny the fact that we are all sinners. Our standing before God in respect of sin is not in dispute, 'For all have sinned and come short of the glory of God' and the universality of death is evidence of God's judgment on sin. We have every right to despise and hate the evil which we have done but in view of the fact that God loves us, we have no right to despise ourselves. Not only that, but in the ministry of our Lord the call to repent, to believe, to follow, to forgive is an appeal to a legitimate human self-interest. It is not selfishness. From a Christian point of view therefore self-interest is a characteristic of man created in the image of God, possessed of a will and a mind, able to make decisions and accountable for them. It is not a consequence of the fall. Selfishness is the consequence of the fall and it is the distortion of self-interest when the chief end of our lives is not the service of God but the fulfilment of our own ego.

The Christian accepts that self-interest as well as selfishness are hallmarks of the world in which we live. It is no use, therefore, designing and devising an economic system based on an unrealistic view of man and for the government to try to manipulate that system for the common good. In this sense the Christian has a sympathy for Adam Smith, who faced up to the challenge of how to use both self-interest and selfishness – or as he put it, self-love – in the interests of the wider community.

> In civilised societies man stands at all times in need of the co-operation and assistance of great multitudes, while his whole life is scarce sufficient to gain the friendship of a few persons. In almost every other race of animals each individual, when it is grown up to maturity, is entirely independent, and in its natural state has occasion for the assistance of no other living creature. But man has almost constant occasion for the help of his brethren, and it is in vain for him to expect it from their benevolence only. He will be more likely to prevail if he can interest their self-love in his favour, and show them that it is for their own advantage to do for him what he requires of them. Whoever offers to another a bargain of any kind, proposes to do this. Give me that which I want, and you shall have this which you want, is the meaning of every such offer; and it is in this manner that we obtain from one another the far greater part of those good offices which we stand in need of. It is not from the

> benevolence of the butcher, the brewer, or the baker, that we expect our dinner, but from their regard to their own interest. We address ourselves, not to their humanity but to their self-love, and never talk to them of our own necessities but of their advantages.[6]

Competition

A second criticism of the market economy has to do with the nature and effects of competitive markets. A nineteenth-century pamphleteer stated the objection clearly. 'Suppose a hundred men produced a hundred loaves of bread. If they piled them in a heap and fought for them, so that some got more, that would be competition. Were it not for that competition the hundred men would all be fed.' A famous Papal Encyclical, *Quadragesimo Anno*, states in a similar vein that 'Free competition, though justified and right within limits cannot be an adequate controlling principle in economic affairs. This has been abundantly proved by the consequences that have followed from the free rein given to these dangerous individualistic ideals.'[7] Competition produces aggression, rivalry, conflict, cheating and discrimination which are anathema to the Christian conscience. For the Christian the ideal is not competition but cooperation, which by comparison produces mutual benefits, modesty and harmony. The above encyclical goes on to argue, 'All the institutions of public and social life must be imbued with the spirit of justice, and this justice must above all be truly operative. It must build up a juridical and social order able to pervade all economic activity. Social charity should be as it were the good of this order.'[8] This criticism then frequently suggests that competitive methods of economic organisation are therefore inferior to non-competitive and cooperative ones, with the implications that collectivism in one form or another is superior to a market form of economic organisation.

In thinking about competition it is important to define it in as neutral a way as possible. In the above criticisms competition is in one case linked to physical fighting and in the other to a 'dangerous individualistic ideal'. Already the odds are loaded against it. It can, however, be defined more objectively. For example, Dr Johnson defined competition as 'the act of endeavouring to gain what another endeavours to gain at the same time'.[9] Within this definition it can be seen immediately that competition is a perfectly general human phenomenon which results from scarcity. It is because the prizes to be won are limited and the resources to be allocated are finite that competition exists. Competition is simply a way of resolving conflicts of interest in society.

It may take many forms: it may be a game of sport, or it may be the violence of the jungle, it could be a beauty contest, an essay prize, or a job interview. As these examples indicate, the basis of competition may be skill, beauty, violence, or just chance. Contrast the violence of the jungle and the skill of the essayist. The violence of the jungle is an important metaphor in economics because many think that the rules by which business is conducted are no different from the laws of the jungle and that existing firms carry on only because of the principle of the survival of the fittest. The point about the business world being 'red in tooth and claw' is that it is a condition without rules in which some are simply destroyed. Consider on the other hand the essayist struggling to win a prize and achieving excellence. In this case the competitors may not even know of each other's existence. What is important however is that we assume the existence of an authority which sets the standards for the competition and which ultimately awards the prize. Notice how different these two situations are: the one resulting in rivalry and the destruction of opponents, and the second taking place in the context of a rule of law.

The economists' concept of competition is very specific. A competitive market is one in which there exists substantial freedom of entry and exit for producers and people. A competitive car market is one in which new firms are free to enter and compete or in which old firms can leave the business. By contrast a non-competitive market would be one in which existing producers set prices by agreement among themselves and kept out potential competition. Similarly a competitive labour market would be one in which individuals could enter and leave particular skills and professions freely, whereas a non-competitive market would be a closed shop where entry depended on being awarded patronage by a trade union.

Sometimes competition may be an end in itself as in a game of sport. But in the economic sphere the purpose of competition is to provide goods and services to the consumer as cheaply as possible. Given the technology of production and the market-determined costs of labour and other resources, a competitive market will, in general, serve consumers more efficiently than a non-competitive market. In economic life competition is not an end in itself but a means to an end. In judging the ethics of competition we have, therefore, to compare the ethics of alternative means and the ways in which the consumer benefits or loses out under alternative systems.

In economics competition is to be distinguished sharply from rivalry. The essential feature of competition is that it is impersonal: the profits of any one firm are independent of what is happening to another. A competitive market therefore implies the dispersion of economic power. On the other hand rivalry is characteristic of a situation in which there are few firms and in which the fortunes of any one firm are dependent in a major way on the decisions of the others. Frequently in the business world the most discredited examples of 'competition' take place under conditions which an economist would describe as precisely the opposite, namely those of 'non-competition'. For example, most price wars are characteristic of non-competitive, not competitive, industries.

It is also important not to confuse competition with criminal behaviour. In certain industries from time to time one reads of corporations being involved in criminal activities such as fraud and corruption and even the use of intimidation and physical violence. No Christian can defend business which is carried on by means of fraud, dishonesty, violence or corruption. But it is a confusion to use examples such as these as either the hallmark of competition in business or as an inevitable consequence of competitive markets.

But all of this avoids the absolutely basic question: is competition Christian? In the Acts of the Apostles the early Church shared their resources together and one of the most powerful biblical metaphors of the Church is that of the human body. Hardly, you may say, examples which suggest making a virtue of competition. These examples go to the heart of the matter. Competition is not a Christian ideal. It is not something to which the Christian community aspires. In a world of perfect Christian men and women, competition would be redundant. But so also would be private property, money, debt, unemployment and inflation. For the Christian, the Church – which is referred to in the epistles as the body of Christ – is a sample of that society. Although not perfect, it is nevertheless wholly inappropriate for competition to be a ruling principle within a spirit-filled community. But the members who make up society are far more numerous than the Church, and society's ethos a far cry from a Christian ideal. The crucial question is whether competition is of value in this situation. Earlier we saw that competition was a method of dealing with the problem of scarcity. Scarcity itself would not be a problem for an ideal Christian world. Nevertheless scarcity remains of fundamental importance in the world in which we live. Although competition is not an ideal for a perfectly Christian world, the case for competitive markets is that in a world of scarcity they are superior to other practical forms of economic organisation in terms of allocating resources.

In this connection all Western countries, and certainly the United Kingdom, have anti-monopoly policies which embody competition as an ideal in our legal system. The Restrictive Trade Practices Court, which is a division of the High Court, operates subject to an Act of Parliament which states explicitly that because all restraints to trade are prima facie not in the public interest, they are illegal. Similarly, the Monopolies Commission and the Office of Fair Trading are constructed on a comparable basis.

Inequality

Another moral objection to the market economy is that it produces inequality which is impossible to justify on Christian grounds. Why should a nurse who performs such a valuable public service earn less than a businessman? Why should a small percentage of the population own a large percentage of the wealth? Why should the rich countries of the world consume a disproportionate share of the world's food? The moral objection is not just to inequality in itself but to the fact that differences in income and wealth cannot be related to differences in the moral worth of those who receive them.

No one can dispute the fact that inequality of income and wealth is a basic characteristic of any market economy. Before we discuss the moral issue however, something needs to be said about the way in which inequality is measured. The typical statistic of inequality which is used in the UK is either that x per cent of the population own y per cent of the wealth or that x per cent of the population between them earn z per cent of the total of personal incomes. It cannot be emphasised sufficiently that these kinds of statistics are open to very serious objections.

Take, for example, the measurement of wealth. For most people one of the most valuable assets they possess is the skills they have acquired through training: what economists refer to as human capital. The greater a person's human capital, typically, the higher a person's income. But any attempt at measuring this is left out of all statistics on the distribution of personal wealth. So are rights to pensions. Yet occupational pensions have a capital value, as do state pensions, equivalent to the discounted value of their likely stream. In 1980, 10 per cent of the population held 58 per cent of the total marketable wealth in the UK. But if one included occupational pensions, the figure fell to 50 per cent; and if one included state pensions it fell to 35 per cent. Then there is the question of how one accounts for publicly-owned wealth.[10] Having access to various amenities which otherwise we would have to pay for is as much wealth as the money in a bank account which could be used to pay for it. The omission of all of these kinds of things makes the wealth statistics virtually meaningless.

Even allowing for the fact that existing statistics of inequality are biased, and even with proper adjustments, inequality would remain a feature of any market economy. The typical libertarian rationalisation of inequality put forward by Friedman, Hayek and Nozick runs something as follows: the market economy is like a game and the definition of a game according to the *Oxford English Dictionary* is 'a contest played according to rules and decided by superior skill, strength or good fortune'. If a society wishes to preserve individual liberty then it cannot dictate the outcome of the game. If it does decide on the outcome, then this can only be achieved as a result of coercion and this of course destroys liberty. For example, if the state decides appropriate income levels for families, those levels can be realised only by taxation or the direction of labour, both of which involve the loss of freedom. The best the state can do is to ensure that the rules by which the game is played are fair, so that fraud, violence, monopoly and other restrictive practices are made illegal. Even in this view however, the state can do more than this. It can also go some way to providing conditions in which there is greater equality of opportunity, while at the same time recognising that it is impossible to achieve total equality of opportunity.

Suppose that the state does attempt to achieve greater equality of opportunity, and also that it pursues a vigorous competition policy, there will still be many factors which give rise to personal differences in income and wealth within a market economy. One is age differences among people.

Even if each individual had an identical lifetime income stream, but the population was made up of people of different ages, there would be inequality in current incomes. Another factor has to do with education and skills. Those who choose to develop certain skills which have greater market value will find that in later life their absolute and relative incomes are that much higher than those who choose not to invest their resources in this way. Similarly, those who choose to save by investing in property will find that in a period when changes in inflation and house prices have been unexpectedly large, they will have a much greater net worth compared with those who chose to save by placing funds in a financial institution. Another consideration has to do with imperfect foresight and attitude to risk. Changing circumstances lead to changing demands for skills, which some people are able to predict and adapt to much more easily than others. Some people are prepared to accept a great deal more risk than others. As a result those jobs which involve more risk (coal mining and stockbroking) tend to have higher returns than those which do not (clerical work and school teaching). Risky jobs also tend to involve greater variability of return; in good years stockbrokers may earn substantial income but in bad years they may end up making substantial losses. Membership of trade unions also influences differentials: it is estimated in the UK that membership of a trade union adds between 15 and 25 per cent to earnings.[11] Apart from these systematic influences personal income differences also result from a host of factors ranging from government regulation, illness, misfortune, chance, natural ability, beauty, intelligence, strengths and skill.

Within this kind of defence of the market economy, differences in personal income have a certain justification, but it is not because they reflect differences in the moral worth of the person concerned. Professor Hayek in many of his writings has taken great care to make this absolutely clear:

> Most people will object not to the bare fact of inequality but to the fact that the differences in reward do not correspond to any

> recognizable difference in the merit of those who receive them. The answer commonly given to this is that a free society on the whole achieves this kind of justice. This however is an indefensible contention if by justice is meant proportionality of reward to moral merit. Any attempt to found the case for freedom on this argument is very damaging to it since it concedes that material rewards ought to be made to correspond to recognizable merit and then opposes the conclusion which most people will draw from this by an assertion which is untrue. The proper answer is that in a free society it is neither desirable nor practicable that material rewards should be made generally to correspond to what men recognize as merit and that it is an essential characteristic of a free society that an individual's position should not depend on the views that his fellows hold about the merit he has acquired. A society in which the position of the individual was made to correspond to human ideas of moral merit would therefore be the exact opposite of a free society. It would be a society in which people were rewarded for duty performed instead of for success. But if nobody's knowledge is sufficient to guide all human action there is also no human being who is competent to reward all human efforts according to merit.[12]

This is a very important point. I well remember taking part once in a discussion chaired by a professor of moral philosophy from one of our older universities on the subject of wages, which included as objects for debate a nurse and a businessman. The question was posed – Why should a nurse who is performing a valuable public service earn less than a businessman? Should not their relative incomes reflect the moral worth of their respective occupations? But for this to be achieved two things would be necessary: one would need someone to state the intrinsic worth of each job; and if it was to be made to work, one would have to be able to enforce the set of stated differentials. However sophisticated job evaluation may become there is no way of enforcing differentials if they depart from those which would be determined by relative scarcity. In a market economy wage differentials are determined by scarcity and not the intrinsic moral worth of the job being done.

Two objections may be made to a defence of economic inequality within a market economy. One is that it takes as given certain inequalities which are arbitrary. To revert to the analogy of the game: some players may be endowed by nature with greater skills than others. Some teams may have superior coaches. Some may have played together much longer. Some may have experience of playing in vastly differing conditions. In the market place why should some earn more than others simply because they are more beautiful, intelligent, vocal, mobile or just brash? A second objection has to do with the nature of private property rights. If I earn so much income why should I assume that I have total and exclusive rights to it? This objection is a quite general one but assumes major importance when put in the light of the teaching of the gospels.

The fact that the libertarian defence of inequality within the market raises problems does not imply that the alternative case, namely the defence of egalitarianism, does not have its own problems. To aim for after-tax equality of income as a major objective of economic policy has three basic difficulties associated with it. By blunting the incentives of economic life to start with, it would discourage enterprise and reduce the real income of the society as a whole. Next, it would seem to many unfair not to allow differentials in wages based on such things as training costs, risk, mobility, hard work, and innovation. Finally, the kind of society which typically decides to abolish inequality of income and wealth ends up creating inequality based on political power because of the discretion which it invests in government.

For the Christian, the critical issue is not the libertarian defence of inequality or the egalitarian attack on inequality but the relationship of both to a Christian view of justice. In this respect I believe that the starting point for the Christian is the recognition of the basic differences which exist in creation and which are thrown into even greater relief by the fact of the fall. One person differs from another in appearance, personality, energy, temperament and ability. The fact of economic differences between people is not defended but assumed in the New Testament. In the parable of the talents[13] which deals explicitly with the issue of stewardship, our Lord makes no attempt to justify the initial unequal distribution of the talents. The same principle operates in the spiritual realm; gifts given to individuals within the Church are not given according to egalitarian principles or even on the basis of merit. Not only is there a fundamental inequality in nature but individual rights to private property are jealously safeguarded by the law. The eighth commandment – 'Thou shalt not steal' – protects the rights to private property for individuals and households by the weight of God's law.

Once we recognise differences in creation and the sanctity attached to property, there is no difficulty about defending the morality of certain kinds of economic inequality in a market economy. Given basic differences of skills, energy and ambition, and given the freedom to work and trade, individuals will find themselves with different net wealth. There is nothing wrong, sinful or unjust about this. This is not to say that *every* kind of inequality within a market economy can be justified. It cannot. But our starting point in assessing inequality must be the recognition that in a fallen world inequality of income is an essential aspect of Christian justice. Of course this is not to say that differences in income correspond to differences in intrinsic worth. The Christian affirms that moral worth is totally unrelated to wealth. The fact that a businessman may earn five times more than a nurse has nothing to do with the moral worth of the respective jobs. The Christian sees his work as a vocation and what matters most is whether before God he knows himself to be doing right.

The Bible, however, does not stop at that point. There are three further emphases which are important. The first is that inequality which results from exploitation, violence and corruption is inimical to a Christian world-view. The next is that justice demands that society should care for those who are unable adequately to look after themselves: in the Old Testament such people include the disadvantaged, widows, orphans and refugees; and in that context caring involves redistribution of income. Thirdly, there is the fact that the Bible emphasises not only the individual's *rights* as far as income and property are concerned, but also the individual's *responsibilities*. It is at this point that the Christian who defends the market economy parts company with secular libertarians such as Friedman and Hayek. Libertarian philosophy makes no demands on anyone to accept economic responsibility for others. But the Christian faith does. The Christian sees himself as a steward of God's resources with a responsibility to use them to help others.

The challenge for the Christian then is this: a certain degree of inequality has to be allowed in society if such a society is to preserve human dignity and freedom and to achieve basic standards of justice. It is important that people should receive the rewards of their work. But at the same time money involves responsibility and the Christian as steward is called to share his resources with others. From this perspective libertarianism is one-sided; it emphasises rights to property to the exclusion of any responsibilities with property: but egalitarianism is also one-sided in that it emphasises responsibilities to the exclusion of rights. The Christian has a perspective which is unique in that it emphasises both rights and responsibilities.

Individualism

A further criticism of the market economy is that it presupposes a philosophy and spirit of 'individualism' or worse still of 'possessive individualism', linked to the writings of such people as Locke, Rousseau, Kant, Howe, Smith and Burke, and results in a society devoid of any sense of community and lacking any concern for justice. For example, Pope Pius XI in his famous Encyclical *Quadragesimo Anno* states, 'The proper ordering of economic affairs cannot be left to the free play of rugged competition. From this source as from a polluted spring, have proceeded all the errors of the "individualistic school".'[14] More recently Professor George Lodge of the Harvard Business School has attempted to show the way in which the traditional ideology of the American business community is based on the Lockean paradigm of private property but results in a society which neglects the unemployed, the inner city and what he refers to as the under-class.[15] At a philosophical level the most impressive attack on individualism has come from the Canadian philosopher C. B. MacPherson in *The Political Theory of Possessive Individualism*, which is based on the philosophy of Locke.[16] He attempts to show that a market economy or, to be more precise, a possessive market *economy*, will inevitably result in a possessive market *society* (because market relationships tend to permeate all social relationships) and that the problem facing any such society is that of generating a sense of political obligation. The ramifications of individualism turn out, therefore, to be pervasive in modern societies.

As this objection to the market economy is a very important one, we need to take care in tracing its theological and philosophical roots. The foundations of modern individualism go back to the Stoics. The basis of their philosophy was that man derives his dignity from being created a rational being, the proprietor of his own person and capacities. Because each individual is possessed of this divine reason, each has the capacity for rational development, and in fact it is this which gives life its meaning. But each individual also has a sovereignty and it is this which makes for the Stoic ideal of self-sufficiency and independence. Like Robinson Crusoe, each individual can realise himself without the help of others. For a person such as this the community is an irrelevance – the only value attached to any communal organisation is if it helps freely consenting individuals to achieve goals which could not otherwise be achieved. This, for example, is the justification of the state. It depends on a social contract. It has no value other than protecting the rights of individuals.

It is but a short step from Stoic philosophy and political individualism to economic individualism and capitalism.

Each individual owns not just himself and his capacities but his property. If the individual is sovereign then private property rights, which are the product and expression of the individual, are sovereign as well. A market economy affords freedom of expression to a collection of sovereign individuals. Hence the demand for less intervention by government and the advocacy of a *laissez-faire* economy.

The roots of this kind of individualism are profoundly anti-Christian. Man created in the image of God does not derive his dignity from some impersonal divine reason but from the knowledge that he, as an individual, is known to and cared for by the living God. As a consequence, life derives meaning not through rational self-development but by establishing a living relationship with the eternal God. Similarly, man does not possess final sovereignty. A person does not ultimately own himself, his capacities or his property. The Bible declares that it is God who is ultimately sovereign and that it is man who is accountable to this sovereign God.

Finally, the implication that the community is an association of freely consenting adults, who can decide to do anything and everything providing no one is harmed, is again foreign to the Christian view of man having been created within a community. The basis of community for the Christian is not utilitarian but part of a created order in which the individual needs others in order to develop himself.

Although individualism is alien to a Christian understanding of man, nevertheless individuality is a part of creation itself and therefore certain of the insights of individualism are valuable. For example, one key assertion of the individualistic philosophy is that there is 'no way of understanding social phenomena but through our understanding of individual actions directed toward other people and guided by their expected behaviour'.[17] In an age which has witnessed the enormous growth of social science and of sociology in particular, this is a fundamental point. A good deal of modern social science, especially that connected in some way or another with Marxism, starts by postulating that society can only be understood if analysed in terms of classes or groups, rather than individuals. From a Christian perspective, however, starting with the individual is a much stronger foundation than starting with the collective because it implies a much surer doctrine of man. The doctrine of man in any theory which sees society as dominated by class, and the individual as being forced to play some role, is a weak view of humanity. It is a far cry from the concept of man created in the image of God. Individualism views man as more resourceful, purposeful, imaginative and rational than does any version of collectivism.

The second key assertion of individualism is that 'many of the institutions in which human achievements rest have arisen and are functioning without a designing mind' so that 'the spontaneous collaboration of free men often creates things which are greater than their individual minds can ever fully comprehend'.[18] This is a considerable insight and of great importance in certain areas. It is of use for example in explaining the growth of markets, the origin of money and the gradual evolution of certain institutions, for instance democracy in certain countries such as Britain. What is wrong however is to ascribe to it a total autonomy in human affairs and to use it through a social evolutionary perspective to explain origins.

A particular distinction which writers of the individualistic school draw is between the individualism of Burke, Acton, de Tocqueville, Hume and Smith on the one hand and that of French and continental writers – Rousseau, the Physiocrats and the Encyclopaedists – on the other, an individualism associated with the French Revolution and Cartesian rationalism. The difference between these views is important. The former sees order in human affairs as the unintended result of individual action whereas the latter sees it as due to deliberate design. The former views man as an irrational and fallible being whose individual errors are only corrected in the course of a social process, whereas the latter views reason as available to all human beings with the consequence that everything of value which is achieved is the direct result of individual reason. One example of the difference between the two views has to do with the concept of economic man. As he emerges from the textbooks of neoclassical economics, economic man is a product of Cartesian rationalism rather than British individualism. In fact, in that man is by nature lazy, indolent, improvident and wasteful, true individualism assumes that it is only by the force of circumstances that individuals can be made to adjust their behaviour.

The distinction between these two kinds of individualism is important. But from a Christian perspective there is an even more fundamental distinction: that between a society proud of liberty, which respects the individual but also accepts responsibility for the community, or a society which comes closer to MacPherson's possessive individualism, the kind of society defended by David Hume, Bernard Mandeville, Josiah Tucker, Adam Ferguson and Adam Smith. I find it impossible on Christian grounds to defend the latter kind of society precisely because it does not conceive of the individual being subject to any responsibility other than for himself. This does not mean that in MacPherson's view a market economy must be defended in terms of a political theory of possessive individualism. In terms of the Christian heritage of Western Europe this is a straw-man which has been put up to be easily knocked down. However, I believe that if one tries to justify capitalism in libertarian terms, as we shall see in the next chapter, it poses a very great problem: namely, how can one be sure that in that kind of society the necessary sense of political obligation will exist and flourish?

Unemployment

The existence of large numbers of unemployed people has always been one of the most disagreeable features of capitalism. From a strictly economic point of view it is wasteful that people who want to work should remain idle. From a social point of view, unemployment is divisive and a source of conflict. From a moral point of view, the existence of involuntary unemployment seems a denial by society of a basic human right, namely the right to work.

Over the business cycles of the nineteenth century, unemployment varied from rates of less than 1 per cent during the peak of the cycles to 10.7 per cent during the trough. During the Great Depression of the early 1930s, it rose to over 22 per cent in this country (in 1932) and to over 25 per cent in the USA (in 1933). It was as a response to this tragedy that Keynes wrote his famous *General Theory of Interest, Employment and Money*, published in 1936, which had such a profound impact on post-war economic policy-making. Whether it was the result of this or not it is difficult to say, but unemployment in this country and in other European economies, such as Sweden and France, fell to very low levels in the post-war years and throughout the fifties, averaging 1.5 per cent in the UK, 1.4 per cent in Sweden and 1.1 per cent in France.[19]

For the past eighteen years, however, unemployment as a percentage of the labour force has shown a trend increase in all Western countries. Given the global nature of the problem it is important, in attempting to explain such a trend, to avoid too simple an analysis in terms of political personalities and slogans about 'monetarism' alone.

There are at least four basic factors which account for the observed trend.

First, the period since the mid-1960s has seen the most sustained and severe peacetime inflation in the whole of our recorded history. This inflation has not only been high, it has also been variable. The combination of high and variable inflation has undermined business confidence and so deterred investment in productive industries and services and encouraged investment in hedges against inflation. As a result, the new capital investment necessary to create extra jobs has not been undertaken. Thus, inflation has destroyed jobs.

This is not invalidated by the argument that a reflationary policy would bring about a reduction in unemployment. I have no doubt that a policy of massive reflation by higher public spending would indeed reduce unemployment, but only temporarily. Higher public spending would have to be financed; and this would mean either higher taxes, the sale of debt and higher real interest rates, or printing money and higher inflation. With one hand the government would create jobs but with the other it would destroy them. We have had three major reflations in this country during the past twenty years and in each case the level of unemployment at the end of the cycle was higher than at the beginning. To argue in this way is misplaced compassion. A far better approach would be steadily to reduce the money supply growth and the budget deficit to achieve zero inflation and balanced budgets (corrected for productive investment) in order to maintain the more stable economic environment which has now been created.[20]

Next, there are the major structural changes which have taken place in the world economy and to which we as a nation are forced to adjust. The emergence of the newly industrialised countries of the Third World, as well as the continuing growth of others such as Japan, have rendered traditional industries, such as steel, shipbuilding and textiles, uncompetitive. At the same time, the major change in the price of oil in the seventies, linked to the discovery of oil in the North Sea, has implied another major structural change for this country. But change means that certain industries contract and others expand and that during the transition unemployment is higher.[21]

Third, is the fact that for a business the cost of employing labour has been steadily rising. In the United Kingdom, real wages grew strongly between 1973 and 1981, increasing on average by almost 1 per cent a year. With low productivity growth and the prices of imported materials rising faster than domestic prices, this meant that labour costs per unit of output have risen faster than prices during most of the 1970s. Labour costs rose 10 per cent more in manufacturing than in the rest of the economy between 1975 and 1981 – the period when manufacturing suffered the fiercest drop in output and employment. Not all the rise in labour costs is the result of wage rises. Statutory charges on employers have increased considerably over the years. National insurance contributions have been raised, the level of benefit offered by occupational pension schemes has been extended, and the cost of providing holidays, sickness and maternity leave has gone up. Legislation has made it more expensive to sack an employee and to discriminate between certain kinds of workers, especially on the grounds of sex. While job security and equal opportunities may be desirable in principle, they are far from costless from society's point of view – a fact that is reflected in the rising unemployment statistics. Other factors which have increased the pressure on labour costs have been minimum-wage legislation and restrictive and disruptive trade union practices.[22]

Fourth, there are the incentives provided by government for people to remain unemployed. Many people are either better off or only marginally worse off out of a job than in employment. This is in part the result of the unintended overlap of the benefit and tax systems: income tax and national insurance contributions become payable at relatively low levels of earnings, while a variety of means-tested benefits, most of them untaxed, skew net incomes so that workers with higher gross pay are sometimes less well off than those on lower rates.

Very high marginal tax rates on low-paid workers have created a 'poverty trap' at the lower end of the labour market and have reduced work incentives.[23] This is not to suggest that the majority of unemployed people choose unemployment over work because of the size of the benefit – though some undoubtedly do – but that those made redundant are likely to spend longer periods of time between leaving one job and starting another, thus increasing the total unemployment figure. There is evidence to suggest that this is happening.[24] Moreover, a housing policy which has subsidised council house rents and discouraged private renting has created a significant barrier to greater mobility of labour between regions within the country.

As a result of these four factors, the level of unemployment has risen steadily over the past eighteen years. The most disturbing aspect is that the future looks grim. Even on the most optimistic assumptions it is difficult to see unemployment falling very much over the next few years.[25]

The fact that the rising trend of unemployment can be explained after the event by economists is however small comfort for the unemployed and does not begin to deal with the moral question. The most damaging aspect of unemployment is its effect on the individual.

From a moral perspective there is one important distinction that needs to be made: that between the right to work and the right to be employed. The right to be able to work regardless of one's race, creed or political beliefs is a fundamental human right. But this is not the same as the right to be employed. The right to be employed suggests that the state has a responsibility to provide employment for all who wish to work. But the right to work is not something general. When people talk of the right to work they mean not simply the right to be employed but the right to be employed in a particular kind of job, in a certain place earning a certain wage. But this is a right which no state can ever fulfil. Even in the Soviet Union the government is unable to provide employment on these terms. The state could provide employment for everyone provided it was prepared to use coercion and provided it did not face rebellion. But as Poland has shown this is far easier said than done.

The problem is that if we are to preserve the basic economic freedoms of our society there is no easy way to reduce unemployment. Creating a stable economic environment for business is a crucial step to achieve it, but a costly one. Since the early seventies many governments in the Western world have been elected to control inflation: Nixon, Heath, Barre, Fraser, Thatcher, Reagan. But the problem continues. Similarly, reducing the costs of employing labour means reducing government expenditure to finance them and once again this has proved far from easy to effect in practice. It also means more flexible employment and apprentice practices and once again this means a radical change in the outlook of trade unions. But unless these fundamental changes can be effected there is very little chance of unemployment falling.

The Moral Case for the Market Economy

So far in this chapter we have considered moral objections to capitalism. It is now time to put forward the positive side. The basic argument for a market economy in moral terms is that with all its weaknesses it is a system which pays respect to human dignity because it allows human freedom. It permits individuals the freedom to buy and sell, save and invest, choose their preferred form of employment, and develop the skills which they feel appropriate. It allows minorities exactly these same rights too. Socialism does not. It pays scant respect to human dignity because it denies human freedom. It for ever restricts economic freedoms. Both systems have been put to the test and we can examine the record. It is vital that in this matter fact should be compared with fact, and ideal with ideal. It is wrong to judge the facts of capitalism with the ideals of socialism, much as it is wrong to judge the facts of socialism with the ideals of capitalism. When we look at the facts, what we observe in one country after another is that when politicians believe (with Rousseau) that people are born free but are everywhere in chains because of circumstances – and correct this by creating a socialist utopia – the vesting of property rights in the state leads to a loss of personal freedoms, the direction of investment, the direction of labour and a totalitarian state.

Imagine that in Britain today the extreme Left were to take over, concentrate property rights in the state through wholesale nationalisation and declare that on grounds of justice, wages were to be equal throughout the economy.

Who would work on the night shift? Who would risk the hazards of coal mining or the rigs of the North Sea? Who would undertake a laborious apprenticeship? In a world in which incentives are systematically suppressed the only alternative left if production is to continue would be coercion. The Gulag Archipelago is the logical end of any red-blooded form of socialism. In practice one need only consider Angola, Mozambique, Chile (under Allende), and the socialist countries of Eastern Europe – not to mention Kampuchea.

The argument for a market economy therefore is that with all its weaknesses, it is nevertheless a system which respects the individual and his rights.

Linked to this is the observation that economic freedom is also an important condition for political freedom. The very existence of a market economy in which individuals have the freedom to own property, to buy and sell assets in foreign currency, to educate themselves, to save, and to change from one job to another to suit their preferences, is in itself an enormous restriction on the power of the state over people's lives. A market economy is not sufficient to ensure political freedom. That must be conceded willingly. But it is difficult to think of countries which have enjoyed a reasonable degree of political freedom which have not also had a free-enterprise economic system.

In this connection an important distinction has to be drawn between a totalitarian regime and an authoritarian one. An authoritarian political system is one in which the individual is denied certain democratic forms of political expression. The government is not voted into office by the citizens or, if elections are held, the public's 'choice' is effectively restricted to the party of the existing regime. Within these limits, however, there is a fair degree of personal freedom. Examples of this kind of government might be Franco's Spain and some of the newly industrialising countries of East Asia, such as South Korea, Taiwan and Singapore. By contrast, a totalitarian regime is one in which the individual is not only denied the right to express political opinions but in which the state attempts to control, through a process of indoctrination, every institution of society: the workplace, the trade union, the school, the Church, the family, the media, the arts. This was the case in Nazi Germany. It is still true of the USSR, Eastern Europe, North Korea, Vietnam, Angola and Mozambique. Many authoritarian societies have a capitalist orientation, but no totalitarian society does.

The consequence of justifying a market economy on the ground of freedom is that a certain degree of economic inequality is inevitable. Even John Maynard Keynes, who was no supporter of *laissez faire*, argued in favour of maintaining a certain degree of inequality for precisely this reason:

> There are valuable human activities which require the motive of money-making and the environment of private wealth ownership for their full fruition. Moreover dangerous human proclivities can be canalized into comparatively harmless channels by the existence of opportunities for money-making and private wealth, which if they cannot be satisfied in this way, may find their outlet in cruelty, the reckless pursuit of personal power and authority and other forms of self-aggrandizement. It is better that a man should tyrannize over his bank balance than over his fellow citizen.[26]

In summary, therefore, the moral case for a market economy is that both in itself and by being a necessary condition for political freedom it helps to protect the freedom and the dignity of the individual.[27]

5

THE IDEOLOGICAL DIMENSION

The final dimension to wealth creation which we consider is the ideological. When Milton Friedman defends the market economy, he is very careful and specific about what precisely he is defending: it is the ideal of a competitive free-enterprise exchange economy. But when the Christian socialist or the Marxist attacks the same system, the attack is not levelled at some abstract economic ideal, but at what is referred to as capitalism. For the critics, capitalism is not the ideal of a competitive free-enterprise exchange economy but the whole social structure of Western societies, divided by class and linked to a set of values and beliefs which, according to the critics, successfully exploits and alienates the individual person.

There are, I think, two major reasons for ambiguity over the meaning of capitalism. One is that the same set of events may be interpreted very differently when analysed from different points of view. Historians, economists, sociologists, philosophers and political scientists look at what is loosely called capitalism from very different viewpoints. It so happens that the most influential of those who have chosen to defend the market economy in recent years have been economists (Hayek, Von Mises, Friedman) while those most vocal in criticism have been sociologists or Marxists. The other is that in this, as in many other areas of life, it is not easy to disentangle facts from values and description from prescription. This is not an unimportant issue, for there is one very important question at stake: namely to what extent the defence of a market economy involves an explicit or implicit set of values. For the Christian, this would become a highly relevant matter if it could be shown that the values which underlie the defence of the market economy are inconsistent with a Christian world-view.

Capitalism as History

We can consider three different meanings of capitalism. Looked at historically, capitalism must be separated from the desire to make money or to acquire more things. To the best of my knowledge the impulse to acquisition has existed in many different kinds of society which have been studied, regardless of whether they were classified as primitive, feudal, capitalist or socialist. By comparison with other kinds of societies, however, the distinguishing feature of capitalism is that within it, enterprises are concerned with the pursuit of profit. A capitalist enterprise is one in which the entrepreneur or management is concerned to evaluate any possible course of action on the basis of a comparison of revenue and cost. In this sense a limited form of capitalism, usually referred to as commercial capitalism, has existed in most civilised societies. For example, Weber noted the existence of this kind of capitalism in China, India, Babylon, Egypt and Mediterranean antiquity. It was a form of system which subsequently developed in Italy in the thirteenth century, in the Low Countries in the fourteenth century, and in England in the sixteenth century.[1]

But this kind of capitalism remained limited. What we today refer to in historical terms as capitalism is that economic and political system which first developed in its modern form in England in the late eighteenth century and which subsequently spread throughout Europe, North America, Australia, New Zealand and South Africa. It was a system which dominated the world during the nineteenth century with its centre at the time being Britain. Then, after the First

World War the UK lost its dominant role in the system to the United States. Over the last few decades, capitalism in its nineteenth-century form has declined in most of the countries in which it originally developed, the most capitalist societies today being the emergent nations of Asia such as South Korea, Indonesia, the Philippines, Malaysia and Hong Kong.

For such an economic system to develop from feudalism, four important conditions were necessary. The first was the emergence of a bourgeois class which produced entrepreneurs, that is, a class of people who were prepared to save instead of consume, and who were prepared to invest their savings in capital, consciously undertaking risk in expectation of profits. Such a class as this did not exist in feudal society, which was made up of landlords, religious orders, peasants and labourers. Next, there was the need for strong government, in order to enforce commercial contracts. Ultimately a modern parliamentary democracy subject to the rule of law was the kind of state which emerged from this system. Third, one needed an element of competition and *laissez faire*; it was impossible to have capitalism flourish alongside the kind of medieval guild system which existed throughout much of Europe. In fact a major contrast between commercial and industrial capitalism was that the latter operated in a world of free labour markets which had never existed in this form previously. And fourth, one needed what the sociologists have termed an organisational economy so that those involved in making important decisions were able to act on the basis of rationality and purpose. This in turn demanded the separation of business from the household and the development of rational book-keeping.

The essential features of nineteenth-century capitalism were based on the precepts of Adam Smith: namely self-interest as the servant of society, the institution of private property, and the minimisation of the role of the state – all of which Smith had argued for in *The Wealth of Nations*. Since the mid-nineteenth century and the coming of limited liability there have been several major changes in the structure of capitalist economies. The size of companies has increased greatly, ownership has been divorced from management and the role played by the government in the affairs of companies has also greatly increased.

Capitalism as Economics

Economists have typically viewed capitalism as an economic system. As such it is an abstraction from both the history of the last two hundred years and from the society of which it is part. From a strictly economic point of view, a capitalist economic system has three characteristics: a widely dispersed system of private property rights, competitive markets resulting from freedom of exit and entry by suppliers and producers, and as few restrictions as possible from government regulations. It is possible to have the first of these – private property rights – without the others. In this connection, it is interesting to notice, as we said at the beginning of the chapter, that Milton Friedman in his various works[2] never defends a form of capitalism which is simply a system of private property rights because this is compatible with monopoly, restrictive practices and many forms of government regulations. He defends competitive capitalism, which is an important difference. For example, there are many Third World countries which have an important element of private enterprise based on private property but which one would never describe as competitive market economies. One has only to think of Mexico, Brazil, Chile, Argentina and Venezuela. In all these examples there is a great deal of privately owned property which gives rise to profits, rent and interest, but in all cases the government imposes strong barriers to new entrants in many markets, restricts trade and foreign exchange and generally attempts to manage and regulate economic life rather than allow the free play of market forces.

The natural outcome of having private property rights is competitive markets unless, that is, the government interferes to prevent it. As we have already seen competition is a strictly defined term in economics and competitive markets are characterised by a number of features: freedom of entry into and exit from the industry; rates of return on capital which are not greatly in excess of those in other markets; relatively low advertising budgets for individual companies; the absence of price discrimination in the pricing policies of companies and the absence as well of cartel and other price and market-sharing agreements among firms in the industry.

The degree of abstraction in economics is greater than abstraction from history and culture. To study capitalist economies in scientific terms, the economist has been forced to even further abstraction. In the real world there are no such things as demand and supply curves or perfect competition. Most firms do not maximise their profits, and it would be difficult to discover an equilibrium price. Most of all there is the assumption of rational economic man, always concerned to calculate the way in which his self-interest is affected by a change in any economic variable. All of these are intellectual constructs which the economist imposes on the market place in order to be able to predict the outcome of expected changes. What impact will a rise in the price of oil have on real GNP in oil-consuming countries? How much will a higher rate of value added tax depress sales of certain goods? At what level would interest rates have to be for money supply growth to be controlled? Such abstraction is of the essence of science and thoroughly legitimate in answering certain questions. For economics, however, the crucial problem occurs when one attempts to apply the result of such theorising to the real world. Abstraction is fine for certain purposes providing one is equally careful about re-integrating the results of this approach for the kind of world in which we live, because the real world is not one made up of rational economic men.

Capitalism as Ideology

One way, therefore, of answering the question – What is capitalism? – is in an historical context; another is as an economic system. Yet another is to consider capitalism as an ideology. An ideology is a set of beliefs and ideas about man, the universe and society, which attempts to explain the kind of society in which we live with reference to such basics as justice, survival and self-respect. It is an integration of facts and values which together add up to a distinct world-view and which can then be used to justify or rationalise some idea or vested interest and simplify political choices. In the 1930s fascism was an ideology. Today communism is a major ideology. Capitalism too has ideological elements to it. Over the past two hundred years or so there have been many outstanding attempts to defend a capitalist economy. What is interesting is that each of them has been firmly grounded in the prevailing philosophical outlook of its time, and that none of them can be considered independently of ideology.

The seminal defence of modern capitalism is to be found in the writings of Adam Smith and it contains an important element of ideology. To understand it, however, we need to look at that great eighteenth-century intellectual movement out of which it came, namely the Enlightenment. In fact it can be said that modern economic thought begins with the Enlightenment. Although its heart was in Paris, the Enlightenment was a genuinely European movement: in France, it involved such figures as Montesquieu, Rousseau, Diderot, Turgot, Quesnay and Condorcet; in Germany, Leibnitz and Goethe; in England and Scotland, Locke, Hume, Bolingbroke and Smith; and in the United States, Jefferson and Franklin. Its leaders and followers saw it as the dawning of a new era, an escape to a new way of thinking, and emancipation from the previous millenium of European intellectual life which had been dominated by the Church and scholasticism.

One of the most penetrating insights into the Enlightenment is found in Carl Becker's book *The Heavenly City of the*

Eighteenth Century Philosophers.[3] For Becker, the Enlightenment can be summed up in certain key words. If we were to ask, for example, which words represent the intellectual climate of the thirteenth century, they would be words such as God, sin, grace, salvation, heaven and Church. For the nineteenth century they would be matter, fact, evolution, progress; for the twentieth century, relativity, process, function, adjustment, complex. For the Enlightenment, the key words are Nature, Natural Law, Reason, First Cause and, for the tender-minded, sentiment, humanity, perfectability.

The Enlightenment was not a wholly anti-religious movement: many of its philosophers were Deists. What the Deists did, however, was to empty the traditional Christian world-view of meaning. They retained religious terminology, but they drained it of its supernatural content. For example, heaven was replaced by talk of the future state and the immortality of the soul; grace, by virtue; God, by a Supreme Being, the Author of the Universe, the Prime Mover, the First Cause, Omniscience, Beneficence. They emptied God of all human qualities as Father: he was reduced to a remote Creator. They went even further. They replaced the Bible and the Church by what they called Nature and Nature's Law. For them the Bible was altogether too small a book in which to gain understanding; they looked in what they called the 'Book of Nature'.

If something needed justification it was enough to refer to Nature and Natural Law. For example, the American Declaration of Independence stated that it was 'to assume, among the powers of the earth, the separate and equal Nation to which the laws of Nature and Nature's God entitles them'.[4] In France, the aim of every political association was 'the preservation of the natural and inprescriptable rights of man'.[5] Holbach, who was an atheist, argued that 'morality suitable to man should be founded on the nature of man'.[6] David Hume in *Dialogues Concerning Natural Religion* puts this into the mouth of one of his characters in defence of natural religion:

Look around the world, contemplate the whole and every part of it. You will find it to be nothing but one great machine subdivided into an infinite number of lesser machines, which again admit of subdivisions to a degree beyond what human senses and faculties can grace and explain. All these various machines and even their most minute parts are adjusted to each other with an accuracy which ravishes into admiration all men who have ever contemplated them. The curious adapting of means to ends throughout all nature resembles exactly, though it much exceeds the production of, human intelligence. Since therefore the effects resemble each other, we are led to infer the causes also resemble, and that the Author of Nature is somewhat similar to the mind of man, though possessed of much larger faculties proportioned to the grandeur of the work which he has exercised.[7]

Carl Becker summed up their view of Nature as follows:

In the eighteenth-century climate of opinion, whatever question you seek to answer, nature is the test, the standard: the ideas, the customs, the institutions of men, if they are to attain perfection, must obviously be in accord with those laws which 'nature reveals at all times and to all men'.[8]

Nature and Natural Laws were not new ideas. They had been emphasised by writers such as Aristotle to justify slavery, and Thomas Aquinas to derive a system of ethics. Even Calvin had talked of natural equity. But there was in their conception of Nature, an element of mystery and danger. But now, because God was taken as being synonymous with goodness and reason, so the natural world too must be good and reasonable: which is why the world is a place of harmony.

For the eighteenth century, natural philosophy was concerned with the description of natural phenomena, the explanation of causes and an enquiry into the condition of the universe. But natural philosophy was not an end in itself: to the extent that it led one to the Author of the Universe, it was a foundation for natural religion and moral philosophy; God could be discovered through his creation. Within this perspective, science is the study of the laws of Nature. If the universe is a machine, the task of science is to study its working. The greatest scientist of the age was Newton. In the introduction to his *Principia Mathematica* he observed that formerly philosophers were 'employed in giving names to things and not in searching into things themselves'.[9] Call to mind Greek philosophy. But to Newton the principles which he was setting forward himself were not 'occult qualities, supposed to result from the specific form of things, but general Laws of Nature, by which the things themselves are formed'.[10] Newton's achievement was enormous. He demonstrated that the universe was rational and intelligible and capable therefore of being subdued to the uses of men.

The eighteenth-century view of the physical world as a machine, which worked according to principles that could be discovered by science, was a world of equilibrium and harmony. But there was one problem with it: how could one explain the discord and disharmony in the world? Pope concludes the first Book of his *Essay on Man* (1733) by stating that the seeming disharmony of the world is but the hidden role of providence.

> All Nature is but Art, unknown to thee;
> All Chance, Direction, which thou canst not see;
> All Discord, Harmony not understood;
> All partial Evil, universal Good:
> And, spite of Pride, in erring Reason's Spikes
> One truth is clear, WHATEVER is, is RIGHT.[11]

What is striking about this is the way in which it shows the remarkable optimism of the Enlightenment with respect to the harmony of the world of Nature.

I believe that it is impossible to understand Adam Smith, and his defence of the market economy in *The Wealth of Nations*, without first understanding the Enlightenment philosophy. Smith was, after all, a professor, not of economics, but of moral philosophy. He never referred to the system he was defending as capitalism, but as 'the system of natural liberty' or the state in which 'things were left to follow their natural course, where there was perfect liberty'.[12] The average or ordinary rates for wages, profit and rent he termed 'the natural rates of wages, profits and rents'. When the price of a commodity was just equal to the sum of the prices paid to factors of production he defined it as its 'natural price'.[13] For him, economic life was part of the great order of Nature and therefore could be investigated in the way in which Newton investigated the planets. In Newtonian mechanics, Nature was a mechanism which possessed order and systematic processes which were made up of various kinds of motion, which in turn reflected fundamental forces. Nature was made up of self-contained atoms which were governed by fixed laws of motion. All change in Nature was governed by these laws. Change itself could only be understood therefore in terms of forces acting within the laws of Nature, creating new situations of equilibrium.

Smith owed a great deal to this way of thinking. He took over the mechanistic concept from Newton and viewed the economy as a machine. Its fundamental unit was not an atom but an individual, and the basic force to which it was subject was not gravity but self-interest – what he called 'the constant and uninterrupted effort of every man to better his own condition'.[14] Self-interest played a similar function to the law of gravity in that it brought together the diverse preferences, inclinations and technologies of economic life. The result was a system which provided an equilibrium of price and quantity and a rate of progress.

From this, Smith then concluded that a society which operated in accordance with natural law would be one based on private property and a market economy in which each individual exercised his natural right to seek his own self-interest. But how did this system produce a natural harmony or equilibrium? Because of the existence of an invisible hand:

> As every individual, therefore, [naturally] endeavours as much as he can . . . to employ his capital in the support of domestic industry and [necessarily] so to direct that industry that its produce may be of the greatest value; every individual necessarily labours to render the annual revenue of the society as

> great as he can. He generally, indeed, neither intends to promote the public interest, nor knows how much he is promoting it. By preferring the support of domestic to that of foreign industry, he intends only his own security; and by directing that industry in such a manner as its produce may be of the greatest value, he intends only his own gain, and he is in this, as in many other cases, led by an invisible hand to promote an end which was no part of his intention.[15]

The invisible hand would ensure that producers responded to, and ever anticipated, the needs of consumers. It was a mechanism which could be relied on to work, provided only that it was not obstructed by government, cartels or controls over foreign trade.

Adam Smith's defence of the market place therefore emerges naturally from the eighteenth-century philosophy of the Enlightenment.

In the nineteenth century another ideology was developed to defend capitalism – the social Darwinism of Herbert Spencer. If the eighteenth century was dominated by the concept of Nature and mechanism, the nineteenth century was dominated by the concept of evolution and progress. Darwin's *Origin of Species* (1850) had a profound effect on intellectual society in the nineteenth century. His thesis was that in the world of Nature new species appear, having evolved from older species. Such a process of evolution results from natural selection, which itself depends on the principle of comparative advantage which he termed variation.

> As many more individuals of each species are born than can possibly survive; and as consequently there is a frequently recurring struggle for existence, it follows that any being if it vary, however slightly, in any manner profitable to itself under the complex and sometimes varying conditions of life will have a better chance of surviving and thus being naturally selected. From the strong principles of inheritance, any selected variety will tend to propagate its new and modified form.[16]

By this he means that if a species of plant or animal differentiates itself in a manner suited to its environment, then it is easier for it to survive. What Spencer did was to take up Darwin's insight and apply it to economic life and that of society as a whole.

The idea that society might be comparable to a living organism was not new. In Plato's ideal society, The Republic, the elements of society were related to aspects of the human mind. The three classes of the body-politic – the rulers, the soldiers and the artisans – were related to Reason, Will and Passion. Hobbes went even further in relating society, not to the mind, but to the human body. Leviathan, the State, was an artificial man in which sovereignty represented the soul; the judiciary, the joints; rewards and punishments, the nerves; wealth, the strength; peace, health; sedition, sickness; and civil war, death. But in view of the advances made in nineteenth-century biology these analogies began to appear rather limited. Both were restricted to the human body rather than to living organisms in general. More important, both considered society as an artificial structure which could be put together like a watch, rather than an organic structure which followed the pattern of Nature.

Herbert Spencer developed a view of society which was an attempt to integrate the latest developments in the fields of physics and biology. In the field of thermodynamics a major breakthrough had been made with the discovery of the conservation of energy or what Spencer termed 'the persistence of force'. The principle, stated simply, was that matter and energy were neither being created nor destroyed in this universe but merely changing form. From the field of biology it could be seen that the form which this change would take was either evolution or dissolution, with the former involving a continuous change from the simple and homogeneous to the complex and heterogeneous. Spencer saw this process at work throughout the entire universe: the earth developing from a nebular mass, higher animals from lower animals, a human being from an embryo, the growth of the human mind. The process had a limit and reached a state of equilibrium in which integration and disintegration, evolution and dissolution were constantly in process.

But he also observed that there were a number of ways in which human societies were comparable to biological organisms. First, they start as small aggregations which increase in mass until they may end up thousands of times greater than they started. Next, they evolve from simple to complex structures. As they grow, their parts become mutually dependent. Then, while individual parts are born and die, the whole survives successive generations of individual units. At the same time he recognised differences: societies lack a definiteness of form; the elements of which they are made up do not form a continuous mass; the elements which make up society are not fixed but free to move; and finally, all those who make up society have feelings, while in animals this is frequently restricted to certain tissue. The differences however were a matter of degree; they tended not to be true of certain lower classes of animals. The conclusion drawn was that while the principles of organisation were similar in societies and organic bodies, the differences had to do with application. Having discovered these principles, he then used them as the key with which to unlock the workings of society. 'There is no alternative. Either society has laws, or it has not. If it has not, there can be no order, no certainty, no system in its phenomena. If it has, then they are like the other laws of the universe – sure, inflexible, ever-active, and having no exceptions.'[17]

All this had a very clear application to economic society. In the simplest of economies there is no division of labour. But with the growth of markets there is increasing specialisation, complexity and interdependence. The principles of growth are similar. In a living organism, growth occurs when there is an excess of nutrition over waste; if nutrition is defective, the result is decay. The excess of nutrition over waste in commercial life is profit. Firms grow from small units to highly specialised and complex organisations when they are profitable. When demand falls and profit falls, firms decline. In other words, the principle of natural selection, or what Spencer termed 'the survival of the fittest', is at work in the economic sphere and accounts for the success and failure of business firms. What economists called competition, the biologists termed adaptation. It is interesting that in the leading text of the day on economics, *Principles of Economics* (1890), Alfred Marshall, its author, who held a Chair of Economics at Cambridge, could say that the advances in biology had given great hopes for economics, and that economists had a great deal to learn from the work of Darwin and others.[18] William Graham Sumner, who was one of the most distinguished economics professors at Yale and a convinced social Darwinist, used the approach to develop a sophisticated defence of free enterprise. Of millionaires he wrote:

> The millionaires are a product of natural selection, acting on the whole body of men to pick out those who can meet the requirement of certain work to be done . . . It is because they are thus selected that wealth . . . aggregates under their hands . . . they may fairly be regarded as the naturally selected agents of society for certain work. They get high wages and live in luxury but the bargain is a good one for society. There is the intensest competition for their place and occupation. This assures us that all who are competent for this function will be employed in it, so that the cost of it will be reduced to the lowest form.[19]

And one of the most successful of those millionaires, John D. Rockefeller, could say in a Sunday School address:

> The growth of a large business is merely the survival of the fittest . . . The American Beauty rose can be produced in the splendour and fragrance which bring cheer to its beholder only by sacrificing the early buds which grow up around it. This is not an evil tendency in business. It is merely the working-out of a law of nature and a law of God.[20]

The contemporary ideological defence of capitalism is libertarianism, associated with the writings of Friedman,

Hayek and Ayne Rand.[21] In particular Friedman makes his absolutes quite explicit. 'As liberals we take freedom of the individual or perhaps the family as our ultimate goal in judging social arrangements.'[22] In this view no person, institution or authority has any legitimate claim over the way in which the individual exercises his freedom. The individual is sovereign and his sovereignty is recognised by his being free to choose. The ethical problem is left for the individual to wrestle with and in this connection two values are important: those which relate to the individual in making a decision and those which affect relationships *between* individuals.

Capitalist Ideology in a Christian Perspective

I have sought in the above section merely to establish one thing: that it is impossible at any fundamental level to separate the intellectual defence of the market economy from a firmly held ideology. Adam Smith was a product of the Enlightenment and his defence of the natural system of liberty proceeded from the assumptions of the Enlightenment view of the world. Herbert Spencer was a Social Darwinist and his advocacy of *laissez faire* was based on an evolutionary concept of society. Today the leading intellectual champions of the free market, Friedman, Hayek and Rand, put forward their case from the assumptions of a libertarian philosophy. Each defence, therefore, is related to a distinct philosophical position: Deism, Social Darwinism and libertarianism. Each defence also presents some image or analogy of the economy which is related to that particular philosophical position: in Smith, the implicit concept is that of the machine; in Spencer, the biological system; and in Friedman and Hayek, the concept of the game. In addition, there is in each a ruling principle which ensures that the system works – this again is derived from its philosophical roots: in Smith, the invisible hand; in Spencer, natural selection; and, among libertarians, chance.

There are many differences between these different defences of capitalism. But from a Christian point of view, despite the differences, they all have certain crucial things in common. *They are all an attempt to present economic life as something which is impersonal, amoral, which can be expressed as a 'system' and which, as a system, has a natural tendency to equilibrium.* In short, they are all derivative of a Renaissance and Enlightenment world-view in which God is pushed into the background and economic life made autonomous of anything Divine or indeed, ultimately, of human as well.

Until the time of the Renaissance, economic life was viewed in *personal* terms. The degree of abstraction was slight, with the result that economic life was not thought of in terms of some system or other. But the notion that the economy might be conceived of as a machine or an organism or a game, transformed the nature of economic life. Instead of the focus being the personalised nature of the individual transaction, it now became the wellbeing of the system itself: the way in which it worked, its efficiency and the conditions which were necessary for its survival.

From a Christian point of view, it is important to see that this concern followed directly from the philosophy of the Enlightenment. As we saw earlier, Deism is a belief in a Supreme Being, an impersonal Spirit, a force beyond man. The God of Deism is the great mathematician who created the world as a complex machine so that it runs according to fixed principles, which may be divined as Natural Law. Having been created as a perfect machine, the world is best left to run according to its own principles. For Adam Smith, God is 'the Great Architect of the Universe' or 'the great Director of Nature' or just 'the invisible hand'. Because of this Deistic view of God, Adam Smith analysed economic life in natural terms: a natural order, a natural price, a natural rate of wages, profits and rent, a natural justice and the great system of natural liberty. By contrast, Trinitarianism is a belief in a personal God, who is actively involved in the world he created. In the Old Testament he reveals himself in the person of Yahweh; some two thousand years ago he became Incarnate in the person of Jesus Christ; at present he lives in the person of the Holy Spirit. The world is not just some perfect machine which can run on indefinitely. Each day depends on the active and continuous support of a personal God who is constantly involved in the world he created. In other words, the concept of an impersonal economic system followed quite logically in Smith's work because of his prior assumption of an impersonal Deity. This is a fundamental point: once we remove a Trinitarian God from our Universe we find it impossible to hold on to man.

By the time we reach Spencer, God is not even the 'Great Architect' or the 'Director of Nature'. He is simply 'the Unknowable'. At the time Spencer wrote, religion was still important in English society and it was necessary that there should be no conflict between religion and science. Spencer therefore developed the doctrine of the Unknowable as a way of reconciling science and religion. Science was the realm of observation, experimentation and the knowable. Science could explain the physical world, the origin of man, the process of human society. Religion was the realm of belief, faith and the Unknowable. Religion had no relevance to the world with which science dealt.

For Spencer as for Smith the natural world works according to laws which are impersonal. In using the 'survival of the fittest' as a way of explaining the effects of industrialisation on English society Spencer was merely observing the inflexible laws of the universe. They were fixed and people had no option but to adapt to them.

While a game might be conceived of in personal terms, this is certainly not the way it is interpreted in Friedman and Hayek. The wealth-creating game of the market economy is not a game like tennis or rugby, or cricket or football. It is not a game in which real people show real feelings. It is a game played by economic men, who might as well be reduced to the fixtures board. The major point about the game is that it allows freedom of choice; it is a positive sum game – a game that creates wealth. But it in no way makes economic life more personal than Adam Smith's mechanistic analogue or Spencer's 'survival of the fittest'.

The other characteristic of post-Enlightenment thinking is that it has removed morality from economic life. Thomas Aquinas was less interested in what determined the market price than in what determined the just price. Economic life in medieval and Greek thought was a branch of ethics. But before one can talk of a just price, one must have some concept of justice. Justice demands that there be right and wrong. Yet it is this very distinction which modernity has done its best to obliterate. Since the Renaissance, everything has become relative. The most that can be asked of a machine is how efficiently it works; or of an organism, of the conditions under which it grows or languishes; or of a game, of what the score is or how well it is played. One must not ask if what is produced by the machine is good or bad; or of the organism whether it behaves morally or not; or how the game may influence the human person. And yet the concern for morality cannot be eliminated. Nietzsche once remarked that: 'Over the whole of English Darwinism there hovers something of the odour of humble people in need and in straits.'[23] Because of his concern that the process of evolution should remain unimpeded Spencer opposed all forms of state help for the poor. Of the poor he said that 'the whole effort of nature is to get rid of such, to clear the world of them and make room for better', and of those with serious physical disabilities he observed: 'If they are sufficiently complete to live, they *do* live and it is well they should live. If they are not sufficiently complete to live, they die and it is best they should die.'[24]

The third element in the post-Enlightenment view is the concept of a natural harmony or equilibrium in economic life. In the pre-modern world order was considered to be established in economic life through the hand of Providence. But when God was removed from economic life so was an ordering imposed from without. In Adam Smith's scheme, harmony prevailed in the economic system because of the existence of the invisible hand. This concept of the invisible hand is a veiled reference to the Deists' conception of God. Individuals acting according to self-interest can be assured that because of the reasonableness of Nature their diverse actions will be reconciled. A concept of equilibrium or harmony in Nature is also evident in Spencer's idea of the 'survival of the fittest'. Evolution is progress to a stable and harmonious equilibrium. The presence of antagonistic forces produces divergent forces which produce the necessary balance. 'Evolution can end only in the establishment of the greatest, perfect and the most complete happiness' and in such a world as this 'the ultimate development of the ideal man is logically certain – as certain as any conclusion in which we place the most implicit faith, for instance that all men will die'.[25]

Rescuing the Market Economy from Capitalist Ideology

From a Christian point of view it is important to recognise that all the major intellectual defences of capitalism as an economic system have been conducted within the context of a thoroughly secular philosophy. There are certain very attractive features to a market economy which we should strive to maintain. But it is difficult on Christian grounds to accept the ideological underpinnings of the kind of defences that we have examined.

First, economic life has to be judged within a moral framework. Efficiency is not enough. It is not enough to say that such and such is necessary because that is how markets work, or that such a result is inevitable because that is an application of the principle of 'the survival of the fittest'. Christianity is vitally concerned with morality and justice, and these are just as relevant to the economic sphere as to other spheres of life. In this area it is economic life which must be made to conform to Christian standards of justice, and not Christian principles which should be bent to serve an autonomous economic order. For example, a business decision must be capable of being defended on grounds of morality as well as profitability. To start with this clearly means that things which are illegal – fraud, tax evasion, corruption – are wrong. The most difficult areas concern issues which have an element of uncertainty attached to them; for example, the nature and extent of corporate social responsibility for such matters as environmental protection, product safety, local community development, and perhaps most pressingly today, the problem of unemployment.

Next, it is important to think of economic life in personal terms. Since the Enlightenment this has not been the tradition. But it was not always so. The Greek word for economics was *oikonomous*, which was derived from *oikos* – household – and *nomos* – law or order. *Oikonomous* was the ordering or the managing of the household, and *oikonomia* referred to the manager. Aristotle in his *Politics* observed that 'the business of household management is concerned more with human beings than it is with inanimate property'. In ancient Greek there was no word for what we today would describe as 'the economy'. The purpose of economics was the welfare of the household and the operation of the household was viewed not in mechanistic but in personal terms. But *oikonomos* and *oikonomia* are words which are used in the New Testament as well as in ancient political economy; they are words which today we would translate as 'steward' and 'stewardship'. It is this dimension which is totally lacking in the writings of Friedman and Hayek and which shows the extent to which we have become the product of Enlightenment thinking.

Last, we have seen that while there are tendencies to equilibrium within the market economy, the kind of harmony which is frequently upheld as part of this belief in the market economy is little more than an act of pure faith. Once again, it is an emphasis on the system, the machine, to the exclusion of people. It is seen in its straight form in the demand for minimal or even no regulation in most areas of economic life. Civil aviation is an area which has been over-regulated in most countries, in many cases through fixed prices to the detriment of the passengers. To suggest however that the government need not be concerned with air safety and to allow complete freedom of choice might eventually produce some kind of equilibrium solution but there might be many who would not live to see it! Similarly the idea that in banking anyone should be allowed to open a bank and that there is no difference in principle between a bank and a retail grocery store, opens up the possibility of all sorts of fly-by-night operators taking advantage of depositors. Of course, in time, some sort of equilibrium would undoubtedly emerge. But it would be after many banks had failed, many fortunes been made and many depositors lost their money.

From a Christian point of view it is imperative that the market economy should be separated from secular ideology. There is much that is of value about the market economy: for the Christian the challenge is to incorporate those aspects within a distinctively Christian ideology. Unless this is done, the market economy itself is likely to be more and more eroded.

Is Monetarism an Ideology?

So far we have considered ideology in relation to capitalism. But equally interesting is the relationship between ideology and monetarism. In the strictly scientific use of the term, monetarism is simply the proposition that there exists a strong empirical relationship between the rate of growth of the money supply and the rate of growth of inflation. It developed as an intellectual concept in response to the inflation of the sixties and seventies, and it has been adopted by governments either explicitly or implicitly, as a way of combating inflation. However, when implemented it has typically involved more than controlling the rate of growth of the money supply. It was considered important that fiscal policy should complement monetary policy if interest rates were not to reach intolerable levels, which meant reducing government deficits. In addition, it was recognised that if economies were to prosper and move, this could only be achieved by a response from the supply side of the economy, rather than by managing aggregate demand as Keynes had suggested. As a result, monetarism has come to be associated with policies for smaller government and a more *laissez faire* approach to economic policy.

From the point of view of ideology, it is the strict relationship between money and inflation which is interesting. The idea that all one needs to do to control inflation is to turn off the tap of money-supply growth comes very near to treating the economy as a machine. It is a simple clinical solution based on solid empirical evidence. At a technical level I believe that there does exist a fairly strong relationship between money and the price level and between money-supply growth and the rate of inflation. Double the stock of money and after a certain time the price level will also tend to double. Similarly, double the rate of money-supply growth and again after a time the rate of inflation will tend to double. Control of the money supply therefore is necessary to the control of inflation.

The problem is that one government after another has tried it, and while it may have worked for a time, no country has succeeded in permanently removing inflation from its society. At this point the typical response of the monetarist is to put the blame on the incompetence of central bankers. However, I believe that the real question which needs to be asked is the extent to which monetarism as policy prescription to deal with inflation is not restricted by an ideology which tends to see economic life in mechanistic terms. Earlier we said that all post-Enlightenment ideologies of the market economy reduced economic life to impersonal and amoral terms in which some equilibrium solution could be guaranteed. In the field of inflation is not monetarism guilty of this very thing?

But let us change the analogy for a moment. Assume the problem is not inflation and excess money-supply growth, but the physical deterioration of the human body resulting from heroin addiction. At a strictly scientific level, there exists a good relationship between increasing the dosage of heroin and the deterioration of the human body. A necessary condition to cure the addict is to reduce the supply of heroin consumed. But that, as we know, is far from being a sufficient condition. If all that is done is to cut off the regular heroin supply, the addict will look for alternative sources of heroin, or alternative drugs, or switch to other substitutes. The key issue, in other words, is not the supply of heroin, but the problem of addiction.

The implication of this for monetarism as a policy to deal with inflation becomes very clear. For nearly four decades, democratic politicians in Western countries have set about raising the expectations of the electorate that real consumption could be increased year after year by techniques of either demand or supply management. In order to win elections, the economy is stimulated: taxes are cut, spending increased, interest rates brought down and extra money poured into the economy. For a time the experience is stimulating: real output receives a boost, unemployment falls, interest rates come down, take-home pay is increased. But after a while reality dawns: inflation starts rising, the exchange rate falls, interest rates soar and the balance of payments deteriorates. But along come another set of politicians, with another set of policies, and the whole process begins again. Meanwhile, inflation has reached a permanently higher level, government expenditure as a proportion of the national income has increased to a new plateau and unemployment has risen to a new high.

As with the analogy of heroin, the fundamental problem is not control of the money supply but the addiction which afflicts the economic democracies of the Western world. To the extent that monetarism is a prescription to deal with inflation deriving from a mechanistic view of economic society, then its prescriptions are very limited because of its ideological foundations. The problem of removing the heroin is partly technical but also partly spiritual. It is to do with a change in will and outlook. The problem of dealing with the inflationary crisis of the Western world is surely similar: at a technical level we know what needs to be done, but unless the problem is seen in a proper spiritual context, we could well have to experience a disaster comparable to the 1930s, or even worse, before it will be cured.

6

THE CHALLENGE FOR BUSINESS

The question we have examined in this book is the legitimacy of business enterprise and the market economy within a Christian framework. It is now time to summarise some of our findings. The market economy with a widely dispersed ownership of property and capital is a far more effective way of creating wealth than state ownership or state control. The evidence for this is overwhelming and can be drawn from countries with widely different cultures, geographies and political institutions. Within a Judaeo-Christian framework the legitimacy attached to wealth creation follows directly from the creation mandate. While materialism, injustice and greed are in fundamental conflict with the teaching of Jesus, there is nothing in Christian theology which suggests that the creation of wealth is anything other than desirable. Wealth creation is not only necessary to sustain life but provides a unique opportunity for people to express their creativity in the service of others.

The moral objections to the market economy were found to hold up as criticisms of the excesses of the market place – monopoly profits, unfair competition, inequality based on fraud, violence and monopoly power – but not as criticisms of the fundamental characteristics of a free-enterprise economy – private property, profit and inequality of income and wealth resulting from freedom of choice exercised within the bounds of justice. In terms of the ideologies which have been used to defend capitalism it was found that many were derivative of a Renaissance and Enlightenment view of man which reduced economic life to something impersonal and amoral, and which at heart was profoundly anti-Christian. A defence of the compatibility of the market economy with Christian theology needs to be very careful therefore to avoid the pitfalls of secularism.

In sum, our conclusion is not that capitalism is Christian. Neither is it that the market economy is the only economic system compatible with Christianity. It is simply that wealth creation within a market economy bounded by a concern for justice is compatible with Christian faith. The Christian businessman should never feel guilty or ashamed at defending the environment within which wealth is created.

Shared Values and Corporate Culture

While the market economy may be defended as both efficient and moral, it does not follow that the basic economic problems of the West can be solved simply by increasing the scope for free enterprise. We have also seen that the root of the Western crisis is not simply the erosion of economic freedom, but the prevailing philosophy of secular humanism. In this situation the appeal for greater economic freedom and the extension of the market economy, while desirable in themselves, are not sufficient to meet the task. The fundamental problem in the West is that we are reaping in economic terms the consequences of decades of secular humanism. An appeal to technical solutions is not enough. It is not simply, in the words of Sir Keith Joseph, that 'monetarism is not enough'; it is also true that 'capitalism is not enough'. More than anything else in the West we need to re-establish certain values at the same time as the market economy is extended.

Since beginning to write this book and taking up an appointment at a business school, I have been impressed with the contemporary emphasis in management thinking on the importance of values within the corporation as an important factor in explaining corporate performance. In

The Art of Japanese Management, written by staff of the Harvard and Stanford Business Schools,[1] and *In Search of Excellence*, which is a study of the most successful American corporations undertaken jointly by an executive of McKinsey and a faculty member at Stanford,[2] the creation of shared values by management is crucial to explaining the success of leading US and Japanese companies. The remarkable insight pro-

Chart 1. McKinsey 7-S framework ©

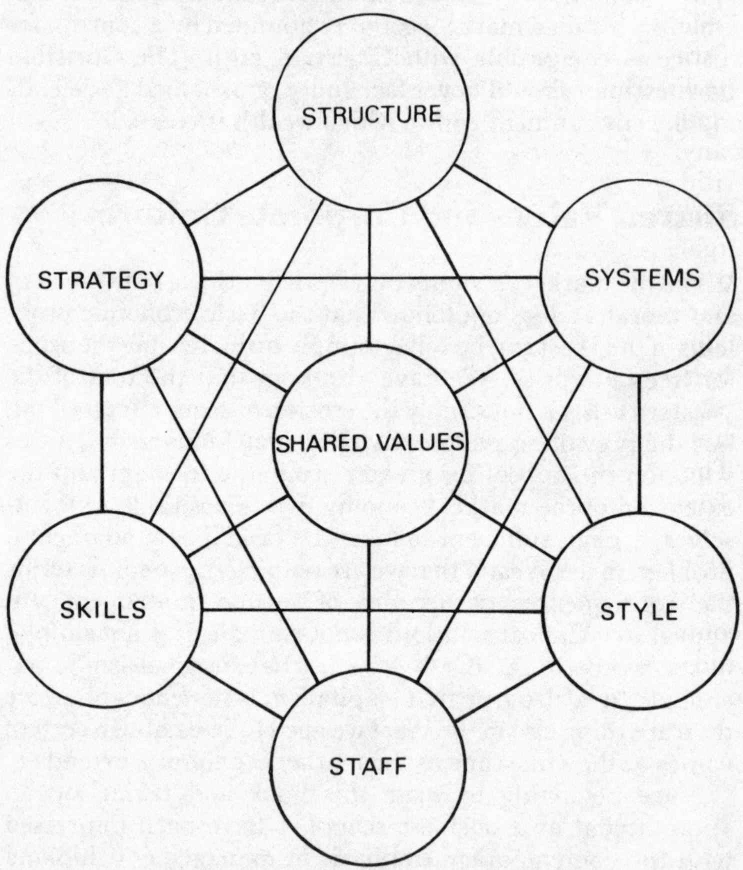

Source: T. J. Peters and R. H. Waterman, In Search of Excellence, *Harper & Row, New York, 1982, p. 10.*

vided by these writers is that the creation of wealth depends on the creation of values. The framework which they have developed for thinking about effective management is a set of seven Ss – structure, strategy, systems, skills, staff, style and shared values or superordinate goals, which has been adopted by McKinsey and which are shown in Chart 1. Each of these Ss is a 'lever' which management can use to achieve certain objectives within complex organisations. Within this framework, strategy refers to the corporate plan adopted to achieve certain goals, which results in the internal allocation of scarce resources to different uses by the firm; structure to the way in which a firm is organised; system to processes and regular reports which handle information within the company; staff to the characterisation of various categories within the corporation (e.g. engineers, MBAs, entrepreneurs); style to the way in which senior management organise their time and the culture of the organisation; skills to distinct advantages of the company's personnel; and shared values to the significant meanings, including spiritual values, to which an organisation and its members devote themselves. Within the organisation shared values integrate every other aspect of management decision-making and the shaping of values becomes the key role of top management. 'The leader not only creates the rational and tangible aspects of organization such as structures and technology, but also is the creator of symbols, ideologies, language, beliefs, rituals and myths.'[3] In the same vein as Andrew Pettigrew, Joanne Martin of Stanford conceives of organisations as 'systems composed of ideas, the meaning of which must be managed'[4] and in *Leadership and Administration*, Philip Selznick is quite explicit on the place of values.

> The formation of an institution is marked by the making of value commitments, that is, choices which fix the assumptions of policy makers as to the nature of the enterprise, its distinctive aims, methods and roles. These character-defining choices are often not made verbally, they might not even be made consciously . . . The institutional leader is primarily an expert in the promotion and protection of values . . . Leadership fails when it

> concentrates on sheer survival. Institutional survival, properly understood, is a matter of maintaining values and distinctive identity.[5]

One of the most remarkable companies of this century has been IBM. The son of its founder, Thomas Watson Jr, wrote a book about *A Business and its Beliefs*, again emphasising the importance of values within IBM.

> One may speculate at length as to the cause of the decline and fall of a corporation. Technology, changing tastes, changing fashions, all play a part . . . No one can dispute their importance. But I question whether they in themselves are decisive. I believe the real difference between success and failure in a corporation can very often be traced to the question of how well the organization brings out the great energies and talents of its people. What does it do to help these people find common cause with each other? And how can it sustain this common cause and sense of direction through the many changes that take place from one generation to another? Consider any great organization – one that has lasted over the years – I think you will find that it owes its resiliency not to its form of organization or administrative skills, but to the power of what we call beliefs and the appeal these beliefs have for its people. This then is my thesis: I firmly believe that any organization, in order to survive and achieve success, must have a sound set of beliefs on which it premises all its policies and actions. Next, I believe that the most important single factor in corporate success is faithful adherence to those beliefs. And finally, I believe if an organization is to meet the challenge of a changing world, it must be prepared to change everything about itself except those beliefs as it moves through corporate life. In other words, the basic philosophy, spirit, and drive of an organization have far more to do with its relative achievements than do technological or economic resources, organizational structure, innovation, and timing. All these things weigh heavily in success. But they are, I think, transcended by how strongly the people in the organization believe in its basic precepts and how faithfully they carry them out.[6]

A very different example is the Japanese company, Matsushita. Pascale and Athos in analysing the firm pay great attention to the relationship between its basic business principles, employees' creed and the seven spiritual values to which it adheres: national service through industry, fairness, harmony and cooperation, struggle for betterment, courtesy and humility, adjustment and assimilation, and gratitude. '"Spiritual" is an unlikely term in a narrative of corporate life. Yet nothing less suffices to capture the strong belief system that underlies Matsushita's philosophy.'[7]

Christian Values or Confucian Ethics

The importance of values as being at the very heart of a corporation is something to which the Christian should be sympathetic. But for the Christian the crucial question must be – What values? In their study of US companies, Waterman and Peters show how a number of values are crucial to successful business. A bias to action, being close to the consumer, productivity through people, hands-on and value-driven management are all important. All of these make very good sense to any entrepreneur. But in the contrast with Japanese companies, the concept of shared values takes on another dimension. For example, Pascale and Athos claim that in terms of shared values, 'what is needed in the West is a non-deified, non-religious "spiritualism" that enables a firm's superordinate goals to respond truly to the inner meanings that many people seek in their work – or, alternatively seek in their lives and could find at work if only that were more culturally acceptable'.[8] From a biblical perspective this statement bristles with difficulties. Indeed our criticism earlier in this book was about the lack of a moral purpose in Western society and the failure of secular humanism to provide meaning in economic life. It is very doubtful if this kind of spiritualism will ever provide a robust enough basis for economic life. We certainly need to recapture in the world of business a vision of what might be achieved but it is difficult to see how this can be done within a non-religious framework of this sort. Secular humanism is, I believe, incapable of providing the basis we need. By contrast, Judaeo–Christian teaching emphasises certain critical fixed points which can serve as the basis for lasting shared values.

First, that the major purpose of life is to serve and worship our Creator and Redeemer; it is only in this context that both life in general and economic life in particular acquire meaning.

Second, that the service of God demands that we be involved in the service of man; this is the ideal of Christ himself who established his Church through servanthood; it is a continuing concept for all in positions of leadership.

Third, we are trustees for everything which God has given us; and he has given us everything – knowledge, skills, wealth, time.

Fourth, we have been created to live in a series of communities: family, school, workplace, Church, parish; and we have a responsibility within these communities to serve and care.

Fifth, we are to strive for justice in the small and the large.

In my view, a concern by executives with these values is just as relevant to the future of business as are tax rates, public spending, labour legislation, the level of inflation or exchange rates. Governments, as we have seen, may produce the conditions necessary for recovery in Western economies. But the recovery itself must come from the business community. Governments may open up the possibility of trade with Third World countries but if jobs are to be created in the Third World, the opportunities must be seized by companies. The onus therefore which is placed on the business community for dealing with our major economic problems is terrifyingly large. I believe that it is only through the renewal of business with a moral purpose that we shall ever be able to meet the challenges facing us. The business corporation is a community. It requires leadership and at present it is desperately in need of a renewed vision of what is possible in business life in terms of the ideals of service, stewardship, community and justice under God. The challenge for the Christian businessman today is to translate the vision into reality.

NOTES

1. INTRODUCTION

1. T. S. Eliot, *Christianity and Culture*, Harcourt, Brace & World, New York, 1940, 1949, p. 48.
2. E. F. Schumacher, *Small is Beautiful*, Abacus Books, London, 1973, p. 36.
3. Pope Paul VI, Encyclical Letter, *Popolorum Progressio (The Great Social Problem)*, published in the UK by the Catholic Truth Society, London, 1967.
4. Jose Miguez Bonino, *Christians and Marxists: The Mutual Challenge to Revolution*, Hodder & Stoughton, London, 1976, p. 114.
5. As can be seen from Table A some free market economies have been successful not only in increasing prosperity but also promoting greater equity in income distribution. Taiwan is perhaps the best-known example of this kind of 'growth with equity'.
6. *World Development Report, 1979,* The International Bank for Reconstruction and Development/The World Bank, Washington DC, 1979, p. iii.

2. THE ECONOMIC DIMENSION

1. *OECD Economic Outlook*, No. 33, December 1983. Table R8, showing total outlays of government as percentage of GDP.

TABLE A. **GROWTH, POVERTY AND INEQUALITY IN LESS DEVELOPED COUNTRIES**

	Decreasing poverty and decreasing inequality	*Decreasing poverty and increasing inequality*	*Increasing poverty and decreasing inequality*	*Increasing poverty and increasing inequality*
High growth	Taiwan (1950s–70s) Singapore (1966–75) Pakistan (1963–70) Costa Rica (1961–71)	Brazil (1960–70) Puerto Rico (1953–63) Mexico (1963–9)		Argentina (1953–61) Philippines (1961–71)
Low growth	Sri Lanka (1953–73)	Bangladesh (1963–1974)	India (1960–79)	

Source: Gary S. Fields, Poverty, inequality and development, *Cambridge University Press, 1980, pp 88–93 and 171–3.*

2. In the United Kingdom from 31.5 per cent in 1961 to 43.4 per cent in 1981; in Germany from 36.3 per cent to 44.6 per cent; France from 36.2 per cent to 46.1 per cent; Italy 28.2 per cent to 38.7 per cent; Canada 26.6 per cent to 38.7 per cent; Switzerland 23.2 per cent to 32.6 per cent; the Netherlands 34.9 per cent to 55.9 per cent; Sweden 33.6 per cent to 59.0 per cent; Japan 20.9 per cent to 29.3 per cent; and the United States from 27.4 per cent to 33.7 per cent.

   OECD Economic Outlook, No. 33, December 1983. Table R9, showing total receipts of government (direct and indirect taxes and social security contributions) as percentage of GDP.
3. *51st Annual Report of the Bank for International Settlements*, Basle, 1981, p. 34.
4. 'Measures of real profitability', *Bank of England Quarterly Bulletin*, Vol. 18, December 1978.
5. See June issues of *Bank of England Quarterly Bulletin*, 1979–83.
6. Estimates of the size of the black economy vary enormously: the figure has been put as high as 15 per cent of gross national product or over £20,000 million. Sir William Pile, former Chairman of the Board of Inland Revenue, suggested £10,000 million. More conservative estimates reckon it around 5 per cent, while others have put the figure as low as 2½ per cent of GNP. In April 1981, the Association of Her Majesty's Inspectors of Taxes gave its own estimate when giving evidence to the Committee on Revenue Enforcement Powers. It said: 'Whether it is 3 per cent, 7½ per cent or more of gross domestic product is debatable, but it is clear that it is large. Both the self-employed and employees are evading tax on a considerable scale. In a perfect world no powers would be necessary, but we live in a world where both petty thefts and large scale organised crime are widespread.' The association put the estimate of lost tax revenue at £4,000 million. The committee eventually announced that it felt 7½ per cent was probably the level

of unofficial activity in the country. (Arnold Heertje, Margaret Allen and Harry Cohen, *The Black Economy*, Pan, London, 1982, pp. 62–63.)

Massive increases in credit fraud have been reported in both the USA and the UK. Bankers and credit card officials in the US estimated that credit fraud in 1982 amounted to $145.8 million. (*Banking World*, July 1983.)

The number of major US corporations engaged in acts of bribery shows that such behaviour is no longer exceptional but involves a significant submajority of *Fortune*'s list of 500 major US corporations. The Lockheed affair (when approximately $9 million was paid out to various Japanese political figures in order to secure a contract with the Japanese airline, All Nipon) was not an isolated case. A three-year investigation by a US Senate subcommittee revealed that during the 1970s the ITT corporation had attempted to subvert the electoral process in Chile (with the encouragement of US government agencies, such as the CIA); the Gulf Oil Corporation had made $4 million of illegal political contributions to General Park's party in Korea; and in Italy there was a concerted plan by the major oil companies for multimillion-dollar payments to Italian political parties in return for legislative favours. Most disturbing perhaps are the findings of a Conference Board survey of business executives in the USA which revealed that nearly half the executives questioned believed that their foreign operations should be governed by the ethical standards of the foreign host country and not those of the United States. Competitive considerations, they felt, should outweigh ethics. Views of this sort have fuelled the US business community's growing pressure on the federal government to amend the Foreign Corrupt Practices Act which sought to constrain unethical payments to overseas governments or companies. The fact that, as a result of this legislation, US corporations have been placed at a competitive disadvantage in the international market place indicates the extent to which bribes and other unethical payments have become an accepted part of business dealing in Europe and other OECD countries. (Y. Kugel and G. W. Gruenberg, *Ethical Perspectives on Business and Society*, Lexington Books, Massachusetts and Toronto, 1977.)

7. In 1951 the total number of people found guilty of or cautioned for indictable offences in England and Wales was 133,000; by 1961 this figure had risen to 182,000; by 1971 to 342,000; and in 1981 the figure had reached 567,000. Violent crimes against the person have multiplied dramatically during this period: in 1951 the number of persons in England and Wales found guilty of wounding, assault and other violent offences was 4,200; in 1961 the figure was 12,000; in 1971 it stood at 26,000; and by 1981 it had climbed to 55,900. The number of sexual offences has almost doubled during the same period: from 5,000 persons found guilty in England and Wales in 1951 to 9,600 in 1981. Crimes of theft, burglary, robbery and handling stolen goods show a similar trend increase: the number of persons found guilty in England and Wales was 115,000 in 1951; 152,000 in 1961; 262,000 in 1971; and 404,000 in 1981. Most disturbing of all perhaps has been the sharp rise in the rate of offending in the under-twenty-one age group:

   A total of 157,000 divorces (absolute) were granted in the United Kingdom in 1981, almost double the number in 1971, when the Divorce Reform Act came into force. Between 1961 and 1981 the rate of persons divorcing per thousand married people has risen from just over 2 to nearly 12, almost a 600 per cent increase. For an increasing number of people, second marriages are also breaking down. The proportion of all divorces that occur in marriages where one or both partners had previously been divorced rose from just 9 per cent in 1971 to over 17 per cent in 1981. Six out of every ten couples divorcing in 1980 had children aged under sixteen. Altogether there were 163,000 children aged under sixteen in families in England and Wales where the parents divorced in 1980, most of whom would consequently live in one-parent families, at least for a while. (Central Statistical Office, *Social Trends*, Nos. 4 (1973) and 13 (1983).)

The number and proportion of illegitimate births has risen continuously: in 1981 over 12 per cent of all live births in England and Wales were outside marriage compared with only 6 per cent in 1961. In 1981 the total number of abortions to women resident in England and Wales was 129,000, an increase of 36 per cent over 1971. (Central Statistical Office, *Social Trends*, Nos. 4 (1973) and 13 (1983).)

The number of drug addicts notified to the Home Office in 1983 is expected to top 10,000 for the first time according to the most recent projections. The figures (due to be published later this year) are expected to show a big increase on the 8,144 addicts notified in 1982. The number of new addicts registered last year with the Home Office has been put at slightly over 4,000, an increase of about 35 per cent on the 1982 figure. The figures indicate the increasing use of narcotics in Britain, particularly heroin. Unofficial estimates of the total addict population (including non-notified addicts) put the true figure at at least 40,000. The projected figure for 1983 compares with 3,023 in 1973 which means the officially recognised addict population has risen more than three-fold in a decade. (*The Times*, 5 March 1984.)

The death rate from cirrhosis of the liver has risen over the past 20 years, with the highest rate in Scotland, where it has nearly doubled for men. (Central Statistical Office, *Social Trends*, Nos. 4 (1973) and 13 (1983).)

For rising juvenile crime figures, see *Home Office*, Central Statistical Office, *Social Trends*, Nos. 4 (1973) and 13 (1983).

8. Geoffrey Gorer, *The English Character*, Cressett, 1955.
9. Alfred Marshall, *Principles of Economics*, Macmillan, London, 1961, p. 193.
10. GEC Annual Report and Accounts, 1983.
11. The argument about the negative impact of increased

public-sector borrowing and employment on private-sector investment and job creation is developed more fully in William Manser's 'Cut "public" over-employment' in *The Journal of Economic Affairs*, October 1982.

12. The significance of increased taxation and government legislation in the decline of employment opportunities in Britain has been demonstrated in a number of studies, including: John B. Wood, *How Much Unemployment?*, IEA Research Monograph, 1972; Robert Miller and John B. Wood, *What Price Unemployment?*, Hobart Paper, 1982; Hermione Parker, *The Moral Hazards of Social Benefits*, IEA Research Monograph, 1982.

    The steep rise in non-wage labour costs in seven major industrialised countries for the period 1970–80 – a phenomenon that has coincided with rising unemployment – is charted in 'How governments tax jobs', *The Economist*, 18 December 1982.

13. Simon Kuznets, *Modern Economic Growth: Rate Structure and Spread*, Yale University Press, 1966, pp. 80–1.
14. Peter Bauer, *Equality, the Third World and Economic Delusion*, Weidenfeld & Nicolson, London, 1981, p. 248.
15. Svetozar Pejovich, *Life in the Soviet Union: A Report Card on Socialism*, The Fisher Institute, Dallas, Texas, 1979, p. 55, cited in Philip Vander Elst, *Capitalist Technology for Soviet Survival*, IEA Research monograph, London, 1981, p. 28.
16. Sergei Prokopovich, Naum Jasny, Janet Chapman, *Real Wages in Soviet Russia Since 1928*, Harvard University Press, 1963, cited in Philip Vander Elst, op. cit., p. 22.

    Jovan Pavlevski, in 'Economies et societies', *Journal of the Institute of Applied Economic Sciences*, Geneva, February 1969, cited in Philip Vander Elst, op. cit., p. 25.

17. W. S. Smith, 'Housing in the Soviet Union' in *Soviet Economic Prospects for the Seventies*, Joint Economic Committee, US Congress, Washington DC, 1973, p. 405, cited in Philip Vander Elst, op. cit., p. 25.

18. Tertullian, *De anima*.
19. R. Mitchell and P. Deane, *European Historical Statistics*, Cambridge University Press, 1968.
20. W. W. Rostow, *How It All Began*, Methuen, London, 1975, p. 31.
21. Max Weber, *The Protestant Ethic and the Spirit of Capitalism*, Unwin, London, 1971 (1905, 1920), p. 172.
22. Max Weber, op. cit., pp. 65, 173–4, 278–80, 282.
23. Christopher Hill, 'Protestantism and the rise of capitalism', in F. J. Fisher (ed.), *Essays in the Economic and Social History of Tudor and Stuart England in Honour of R. H. Tawney*, Cambridge University Press, 1961, p. 39.
24. This is not to say that 'the essential thread has suddenly been discovered which would lead dialectically from the nailing of Luther's ninety-five theses on the Wittenburg church door to the assembly lines of Detroit and the ramifications of Standard Oil' (Herbert Luethy, 'Once again: Calvinism and capitalism', *Encounter*, No. 22, 1964, pp. 28–9). It is a 'spirit of capitalism' and not the capitalist system, which is related causally to Protestantism in Weber's writings.

    'We have no intention whatever,' he writes, 'of maintaining such a foolish and doctrinaire thesis as that the spirit of capitalism . . . could only have arisen as the result of certain effects of the Reformation, or even that capitalism as an economic system is a creation of the Reformation. In itself, the fact that certain important forms of capitalist business organisation are known to be considerably older than the Reformation is a sufficient refutation of such a claim. On the contrary, we only wish to ascertain whether and to what extent religious forces have taken part in the qualitative formation and the quantitative expansion of that spirit over the world . . . In view of the tremendous confusion of interdependent influences between the material basis, the forms of social and political organisation, and the ideas current in the time of the Reformation, we can only proceed by investigating whether and at what points certain correlations between forms of religious belief and practical ethics can be worked out.' (Weber, op. cit., pp. 91–2.)

He insisted that a particular economic ethic could exist independently of its objective manifestation in a corresponding economic form or system, and that the origins of the latter must therefore be investigated separately from the former. Nevertheless, he believed that in practice economic spirit and economic form tended to develop an 'elective affinity' for each other. By suggesting an elective affinity between Protestant teachings and the capitalist mentality, he would seem to be claiming that there is a 'convergence' or 'resonance' between the ideas expressed in the former and the interest implicit in the latter, and not that the Protestant ethic actually created or explains the nature of the modern capitalist world-view, let alone the forms of industrial capitalism as they developed in Western Europe.

Interestingly, Tawney, having initially set out to challenge some of Weber's arguments, arrived eventually at a not dissimilar conclusion. 'In [Tawney's] view, it was the gradual abdication by religion of the spheres of economic and political activity – a secularisation of the business world that was coincidental with, but not the consequence of the Reformation – which permitted the rise of unrestrained capitalist individualism. At the same time, aspects of Calvinist teaching that were in harmony with the entrepreneurial and individualistic mentality of the bourgeoisie were readily employed by post-Restoration businessmen as a convenient justification for economic enterprise, and in this way helped further their activities. Early Puritanism, following the teachings of Calvin, had displayed a dual ethic of individualism and social obligation. The ascendant middle classes selected from it only those elements which were suited to their purposes, namely those emphasising the ethic of individualism. They conveniently ignored the ethic of social accountability and as can be seen from the teachings of post-Restoration Puritans, in this way usurped the theology for their own ends. By the nineteenth century, this process had reached the point where the business world was totally secularised and the individualistic elements of Protestant theology had given way entirely to the egoism of Samuel Smiles.' (Gordon Marshall, *In Search of the Spirit of Capitalism*, Hutchinson, 1982, p. 202.)

25. For example, in his study of a Mexican village, *Tzintzuntan* (Little, Brown, Boston, 1967), G. M. Foster, an American anthropologist, shows how a certain perception of wealth discourages attempts at self-improvement. The villagers believe that there is limited good and hence any person's gain must represent another's loss. The existing balance must be maintained, so individuals who try to accumulate wealth or improve their social and economic position are stigmatised as anti-social. Those who prosper are expected to channel their resources into the sponsorship of the fiesta system, an institution which contributes much to an egalitarian social structure but little to economic development. In another study, *Politics, Personality and Nation-building* (Yale University Press, New Haven, London, 1962), Lucien Nye attempts to explain the failure of development in Burma in terms of the absence of such crucial values as security, trust and decisiveness.

In Weber's other two major works in this field – *The Religion of India* and *The Religion of China* – he contrasts Calvinistic values with those of Hinduism, Confucianism and Taoism, and seeks to discover the relationship between these different value systems and the socio-economic systems of India and China. And in *The Moral Basis of a Backward Society* (University of Chicago Press, Chicago, 1958), Edward Banfield attempts to explain the backwardness of a south Italian village in terms of the average family's exclusive concern with the short-term interests of its own members and of its perception of the outside world as a hostile environment in which other nuclear families will behave in a similar fashion.

With regard to private property rights, Paul Harrison makes some interesting observations about the way in which traditional, communal forms of land tenure have acted as a brake on technological progress among the impoverished nomadic and farming tribes of West Africa. 'Management of the herds and ranges could be vastly improved: the whole of the ranges could be replanted with pasture legumes . . . [which] provide a good feed, resist trampling and maintain soil fertility. But the ranges are communal property and no one really owns them. No one has any direct incentive to improve them . . . The African way of landholding has many virtues. As one often-quoted Nigerian chief poetically remarked: "The land belongs to a big family of which many members are dead, some are living, and innumerable others are still to be born." In the traditional view, a man cannot own the land, because he did not make it: it was always there, a gift from the gods, in trust for the lineage. A man can own the fruit of the earth – crops and trees which he himself planted and tended. But he cannot dispose of his plot or sell it, there is no individual title to land, no market in real estate . . . Land is usually allocated by village chiefs, and each family is given as much as its members need to cultivate. There is no question of anyone getting extra and farming it with hired labourers . . . For social justice this system could hardly be improved upon. But it has a major drawback from the technological point of view. If a man does not own his land, and indeed even shifts his plots regularly, he has no incentive to make permanent improvements or investments in the land, such as erosion control or irrigation. There is no stimulus for technical innovation . . . With a population greater than existing technology can support from the land, it [has] become a matter of life and death.' (Paul Harrison, *Inside the Third World*, Penguin, 1979, 1981, pp. 72–4.)

In spite of the apparent similarities, the West African concept of holding the land in trust as a gift of the gods is in fact fundamentally different from the Old Testament concept of stewardship, in which trustee property rights were ultimately vested in individual families rather than the whole tribe and which, within the limits set by the Sabbath and Jubilee laws, allowed for a market in real estate.

26. There exists prima facie evidence to suggest that different groups of people in Third World situations faced with a similar environment, similar opportunities and a similar form of economic organisation, but with different cultural values, tend to perform differently in economic terms. Within Nigeria the performance of the Ibos has been noticeably superior to that of other tribes; in Malaysia the Chinese have tended to be far more enterprising than the Malays; in East Africa the Indian population has shown more resourcefulness than the indigenous African population; and in India the Sikhs in the Punjab have experienced something of an economic miracle which is in marked contrast to the Muslim Bengalis.

The last of these is particularly interesting. The Sikhs were moved to the Punjab after partition in 1947. Farm production increased rapidly, major new initiatives were taken in irrigation and infrastructure; in the 1960s there was an enormous surge in agricultural output – wheat production trebled between 1966–7 and 1970–1, the rice crop increased from 280,000 tonnes in 1965–6 to 1.9 million tonnes in 1973–4. This is in marked contrast to the stagnation associated with the caste system in other areas of India. Sikhs in Ludhiana have no doubt that without the Sikh character the development would never have taken place. One has said: 'I think it had something to do with our religion.' In his monograph, *Green Revolution in the Punjab* (Punjab Agricultural University, Ludhiana, 1975, p. 5), M. S. Rhandhawa says:

> Sikhism is a faith which brought about a social revolution in north India five centuries ago. It broke the fetters of the

caste system and provided an equal opportunity to the oppressed and the down-trodden to attain human dignity. It liberated people from the ancient Brahminical system which looked to the past for its Golden Age. The new faith promoted dignity of labour and exhorted its followers to earn their living by manual work. Its ban on smoking promoted physical fitness. Above all, it gave new dignity to agriculture which was declared the best of professions. The system of the common kitchen which provided free meals also had a levelling influence.

27. William A. P. Manser, 'Public industry and public pay', *The Banker*, December 1981.
28. The Report on the Independent Commission on International Development Issues under the Chairmanship of Willy Brandt, *North–South: A Programme for Survival*, Pan Books, London, 1980, p. 25.
29. Brian May, *The Third World Calamity*, Routledge & Kegan Paul, London and Henley, 1981.
30. Niels Mulder, *Mysticism and Everyday Life in Contemporary Java*, Singapore University Press, 1978, p. 98.
31. Maxime Rodinson, *Islam and Capitalism*, Allen Lane, London, 1974, p. 92.
32. Brian May, op. cit., pp. 207–11.
33. Niels Mulder, op. cit., p. 162.
34. Alexander Solzhenitsyn, 'Commencement Address' at Harvard University, 8 June 1978, in *Alexander Solzhenitsyn speaks to the West*, Bodley Head, London, 1978, pp. 595–6.

3. THE THEOLOGICAL DIMENSION

All biblical references are from the Revised Standard Version unless otherwise stated.

1. Luke 18:24.
2. Matthew 6:19.
3. Luke 6:20.

4. Luke 6:24.
5. Luke 12:15.
6. Matthew 6:24.
7. Matthew 19:24.
8. Luke 18:22.
9. Luke 5:11.
10. Luke 6:30.
11. Luke 14:33.
12. 2 Corinthians 8:9.
13. Conrad Boema, *Rich Man, Poor Man and the Bible*, SCM, London, 1979, p. 50.
14. Parable of the talents – Matthew 25:14–30. Parable of the pounds – Luke 19:11–27. Parable of the unjust steward – Luke 16:1–13.
15. Provision for parents – Matthew 15:3–9. Charitable giving – Matthew 6:2–4.
16. Dinner invitations – Luke 11:37; Luke 14:1; Luke 5:29. Use of friends' resources – Luke 8:3; Mark 1:29–31; Mark 3:9. Zacchaeus – Luke 19:1–10.
17. Matthew 6:33 (King James Version).
18. E. P. Scott, *Ethical Teaching of Jesus*, Macmillan, New York, 1924, quoted in R. E. O. White, *Biblical Ethics*, The Paternoster Press, Exeter, 1979, p. 79.
19. Luke 4:18–19.
20. Luke 12:17–21.
21. Luke 16:19–31.
22. Luke 6:20; Matthew 5:3.
23. Luke 16:11.
24. Matthew 25:31–46.
25. Colossians 1:15–17.
26. Hebrews 1:2–3.
27. Genesis 1:12.
28. Psalms 19, 33, 104, 148, for example.
29. Genesis 1:28.
30. Genesis 2:15.
31. Acts 18:1–4; 1 Corinthians 9:6–18; 2 Thessalonians 3:7–9.
32. 2 Thessalonians 3:10–12.

33. Exodus 22:1 and 21:16.
34. Re-allocation of titles – Leviticus 25:1–7, 8–34 and 42–55. Restrictions on capital markets – Leviticus 25:35–8 and Deuteronomy 23:19–20.
35. The Promised Land was first divided into territories on a tribe-by-tribe basis, then into towns and villages (with their surrounding lands) on a clan-by-clan basis, and finally into fields and vineyards (with houses) on a family-by-family basis. The concept of family property occurs several times in Leviticus 25 and 27, and again forms the basis of the charge against Ahab when he sought to dispossess Naboth of his inheritance (1 Kings 21).
36. Leviticus 25:14–17 and 25–34.
37. Leviticus 25; Deuteronomy 15:1–11.
38. Leviticus 25:23 (New International Version).
39. Deuteronomy 23:19–20; Leviticus 25:35–8.
40. Matthew 20: 14–15.
41. Deuteronomy 10:17–18.
42. Sabbath Year and Year of Jubilee – Leviticus 25. Gleaning laws – Leviticus 19:9–10; Leviticus 23:22. Tithes – Deuteronomy 14:22–9. Prohibition of usury – Deuteronomy 23:19–20; Leviticus 25:35–8. Collateral not to be demanded – Exodus 22:26–7; Deuteronomy 24:10–13. Treatment of slaves – Deuteronomy 15:12–17.
43. Amos 2:6–9; Amos 5:7–12; Amos 8:4–6; Isaiah 5:7–23.
44. In setting out the challenge of the divine mandate to exercise dominion over the physical world and to be involved in the process of wealth creation, it is also necessary to remember that 'even in the Garden of Eden, the cultural mandate was not man's noblest calling. Adam was called to walk and talk with the living God. Intimate communion with the most high God is itself the deepest want of the human heart and the highest dignity of human existence.' (Walter J. Chantry, *God's Righteous Kingdom*, Banner of Truth Trust, Edinburgh, 1980, p. 23.)
45. Luke 17:20–1.

46. Saint Augustine, *The City of God*, Everyman's Library, Dent/Dutton, London and New York, 1945.

4. THE MORAL DIMENSION

1. See Martin J. Wiener, *English Culture and the Decline of the Industrial Spirit: 1850–1980* (Cambridge University Press, 1981), for a thorough examination of the pervasive hostility towards industrialism and economic growth among the English literary elite and the upper and middle classes more generally.
2. Robert Blatchford, *Merrie England*, London, 1894, p. 21.
3. R. H. Tawney, *Religion and the Rise of Capitalism*, Merton Books, 1960, p. 235.
4. Joan Robinson, *Freedom and Necessity*, Allen & Unwin, 1970, p. 111.
5. St Bernard of Clairvaux, cited in William A. Spumer, *Ethics and Business*, Charles Scribner & Sons, New York, 1962.
6. Adam Smith, *The Wealth of Nations*, Methuen, London, 1961, Vol. I, p. 18.
7. Pope Pius XI, *Quadragesimo Anno*, p. 88.
8. Ibid.
9. *Oxford Dictionary*.
10. Central Statistical Office, *Social Trends*, No. 123, 1983, HMSO.
11. Study by Layard, Metcalf & Nickell, cited in Brian Griffiths, 'The economics of labour power: can trades unions raise real wages?', in *Trade Unions: Public Goods or Public 'Bads'?*, IEA Readings 17, London, 1978.
12. F. A. Hayek, *The Constitution of Liberty*, Routledge & Kegan Paul, London, 1960, pp. 93–4.
13. Matthew 25: 14–30.

14. Pope Pius XI, op. cit., p. 88.
15. George Lodge, *The New American Ideology*, Alfred A. Knopf, New York, 1976.
16. C. B. MacPherson, *The Political Theory of Possessive Individualism: Hobbes to Locke*, Oxford University Press, 1962.
17. F. A. Hayek, *Individualism and Economic Order*, Routledge & Kegan Paul, London, 1948, p. 10.
18. Ibid., p. 107.
19. William Ashworth, *An Economic History of England: 1870–1939*, Methuen, London, 1960, pp. 25, 37, 98 and 194.
20. For a more detailed discussion of the effects of inflation on unemployment, see: Brian Griffiths, *Inflation: The Price of Prosperity*, Weidenfeld & Nicolson, London, 1976. The relationship between unemployment and inflation has also been analysed in depth by Milton Friedman and F. A. Hayek. See Milton Friedman, *The Optimum Quantity of Money*, Macmillan, 1969; Milton Friedman, *Inflation and Unemployment: The New Dimension of Politics*, IEA Occasional Paper 51, Institute of Economic Affairs, 1977; F. A. Hayek, *Full Employment at Any Price?*, IEC Occasional Paper 45, Institute of Economic Affairs, 1975; F. A. Hayek, *1980s Unemployment and the Unions*, Hobart Paper 87, Institute of Economic Affairs, 1980. Friedman's and Hayek's main arguments have been well summarised by Robert Miller and John B. Wood in *What Price Unemployment? An Alternative Approach*, Hobart Paper 92, Institute of Economic Affairs, 1982.
21. A detailed examination of the effect of Third World industrial development on employment in the West is made in Michael Beenstock, *The World Economy in Transition*, Allen & Unwin, 1983.

His basic argument is that unemployment in the developed countries fell until 1966. During the second half of the 1960s this trend was reversed and unemployment began to rise. During the 1970s it rose sharply and the OPEC oil-price hikes of 1973–4 contributed to the subsequent growth of unemployment. As far as the transition factor is concerned, the most important feature is that a structural break in the behaviour of employment in the developed countries occurred well before the OPEC oil-price hikes and well before the resurgence of inflation in the early 1970s. The seeds of the unemployment in the 1970s were sown in the second half of the 1960s.

This would seem to be closely related to the economic expansion which took place in the LDCs (less developed countries) around the mid-1960s as they industrialised. The result of high growth rates in industrial production and manufacturing output in the developing market economies from 1963 to 1973 was a disproportionate increase in the supply of manufactured products. This caused the relative price of manufactures on world markets to decline. This relative price shift reduced economic incentives in the West with respect to the production of manufactures, triggering de-industrialisation across the OECD as a whole. This was accompanied by increased competition in manufactures on the part of LDCs in OECD markets. Industrialisation in the LDCs raised the rate of return on capital relative to the rate of return on capital in OECD countries. This induced the export of capital from the OECD bloc to the LDCs, lowering OECD investment and raising LDC investment. Consequently, productivity growth in developed countries was reduced.

As OECD economies adjust to the change in relative prices and lower capital stock, structural unemployment has grown. It takes time before redundant steelworkers can move into other occupations. In certain sectors labour is scarce while in the manufacturing sector there is an excess supply of labour. This can be termed 'mismatch' unemployment. It is not a paradox but an implication of the transition that is taking place in the balance of the world economy. Once the transition is complete, mismatch unemployment should disappear, although protectionist policies could prolong the necessary adjustment.

22. In 1981 *The Midland Bank Review* published an analysis of the impact on employment of rising wage costs in manufacturing industry.

The total cost per unit of labour employed is related to output per employee in manufacturing, and then to the 'value-added' price the manufacturer receives per unit of output. This is called the 'real product wage' and is plotted in Chart A as a five-year moving average since 1950. The index of 'real product wages' is then plotted against the volume of employment. It is, as the *Review* says, the real product wage which will influence the employer's decision as to whether or not he can offer more employment. The chart shows that the manufacturer's ability to offer employment has been declining since the middle 1960s, as the real product wage has increased or, to put it in other words, as his ability to pay his wage bill, to cover his other costs and to make a profit has decreased.

In manufacturing industry the share of rising labour costs represented by wages and salaries alone has fallen from just over 91 per cent in 1968 to 82 per cent in 1981. National insurance contributions have risen from 4.4 per cent to over 9 per cent during the same period. It is difficult to assess the precise effect on incentives and job opportunities of employment protection legislation but its effect is clearly in the same direction as the more easily quantifiable employers' NIC burden. 'Its most onerous provisions are probably those related to "unfair dismissal", making companies reluctant to dismiss even unsatisfactory employees and keen to reduce the number of employees they take on, for fear of getting a troublemaker and having to go through an Industrial Tribunal. If you cannot sack, you do not recruit.' High national insurance contributions and employment protection legislation have the undesirable effect not only of inflating the gross costs to employers but at the same time reducing the net wages of employees (see note 25), thereby reducing both the demand for labour and its

Chart A.
Real product wage and employment in UK manufacturing (1975 = 100)
(Average of five years ending in year shown)

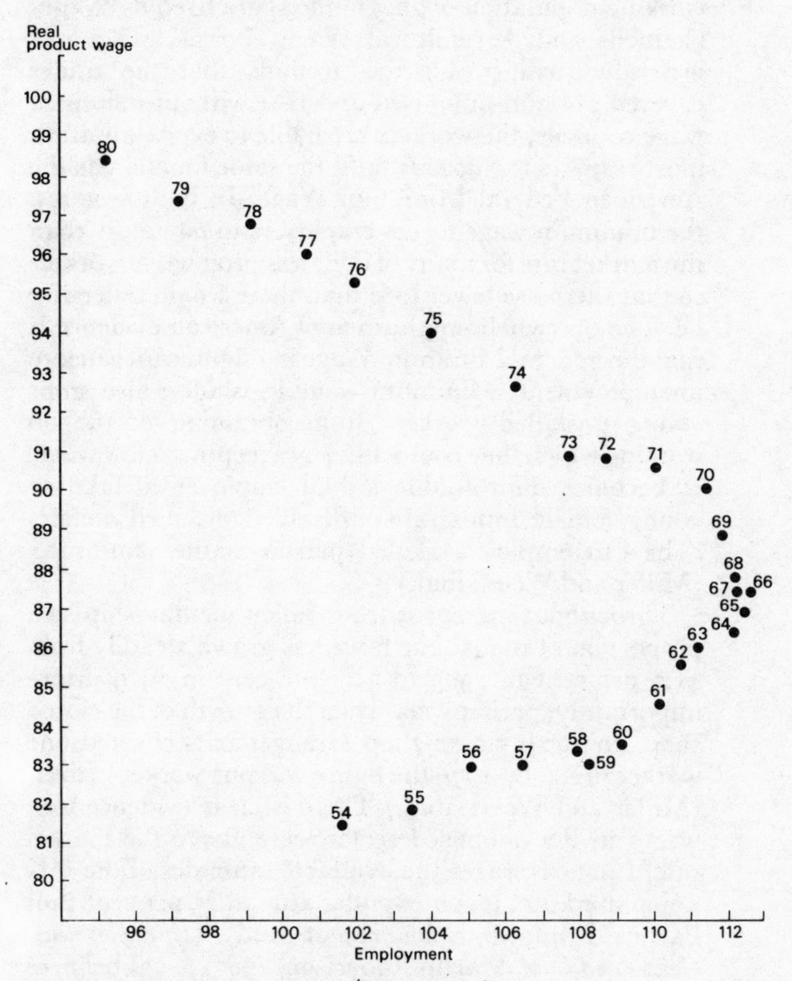

[Midland Bank Review, Autumn/Winter 1981]

supply. (Robert Miller and John B. Wood in *What Price Unemployment? An Alternative Approach*, Hobart Paper 92, Institute of Economic Affairs, 1982.)

The wages of nearly 3½ million workers (out of a working population of 26.3 million) are fixed by Wages Councils and Agricultural Wages Boards. They are generally justified on the grounds that the trades covered are non-unionised and that without unions or wage councils, the workers are liable to exploitation. In most respects the boards fulfil the same function as the American Federal Minimum Wage. In both systems, the minimum wage forces employers to pay more than the market rate for many of their less productive workers so that there are fewer jobs than there would otherwise be. The overwhelming burden of American evidence is that the Federal Minimum Wage is a significant cause of unemployment. Minimum wage legislation also stops young unskilled workers from obtaining on-the-job training which they could 'buy' by accepting a low wage. It becomes unprofitable for an employer to take on young, female, immigrant or disabled unskilled workers if he can employ a skilled person at the same rate. (Miller and Wood, ibid.)

Throughout the 1970s trade union membership as a proportion of the labour force has grown steadily from 41.3 per cent in 1969 to 51.2 per cent in 1979. More importantly, perhaps, has been the growth of the closed shop. In 1964, closed-shop arrangements covered one worker in six; by 1979 the figure was one worker in four. (Miller and Wood, ibid.) There is clear evidence that wages in the unionised sector were above the market rate. If one averages the available estimates of the UK union mark-up, it comes out at around 25 per cent. But Patrick Minford in his recent study (*Unemployment: Causes and Cure,* Martin Robertson, 1983, p. 25) believes that this is downward biased and tentatively estimates a figure of 70 per cent. It follows that insofar as the unions can and do set wages above the market rate they will tend to cause or perpetuate unemployment. National wage bargaining also affects unemployment as it sets wages without any adjustment for the relative value of the same work in different parts of the economy and the country. This concentrates unemployment in areas where employers cannot pay the national rates because they cannot pass them on to the consumers in higher prices. The upward pressure on costs is further intensified by the unions' insistence on unjustifiably long periods of apprenticeship and by other methods of restricting new entrants to the industry. Minford estimates that a fall of one percentage point in the unionisation rate (the proportion of workers who are members of trade unions) would have cut real wages by 0.8 per cent in 1980 and reduced unemployment by 170,000.

23. Since 1980 the situation regarding financial work incentives for the lower paid has deteriorated as is illustrated in Chart B. Using a computer model developed at the City University Business School, it shows how the relationship between a family's disposable income and the number of hours worked has changed during the four-year period from 1979 to 1983 (post budget). The family 'budget lines' are determined by the interplay of wage rates, taxation and social security arrangements. An upward-sloping budget line means that an increase in the number of hours worked is reflected in an increase in disposable income. A downward-sloping budget line signifies a person made worse off by working more hours. Where the budget line is flat (the 'poverty trap'), it does not make economic sense for an individual to work more, although of course he may choose to do so for other, non-financial reasons.

The flat section in both budget lines is caused by an implicit marginal tax rate of 100 per cent in supplementary benefit receipts. Between 1979 and 1980 the length and the level of the 'supplementary benefit plateau' increased, thus weakening economic work incentives. Since 1983, the withdrawal of Family Income

Chart B
Budget lines of a married man with two children – low pay

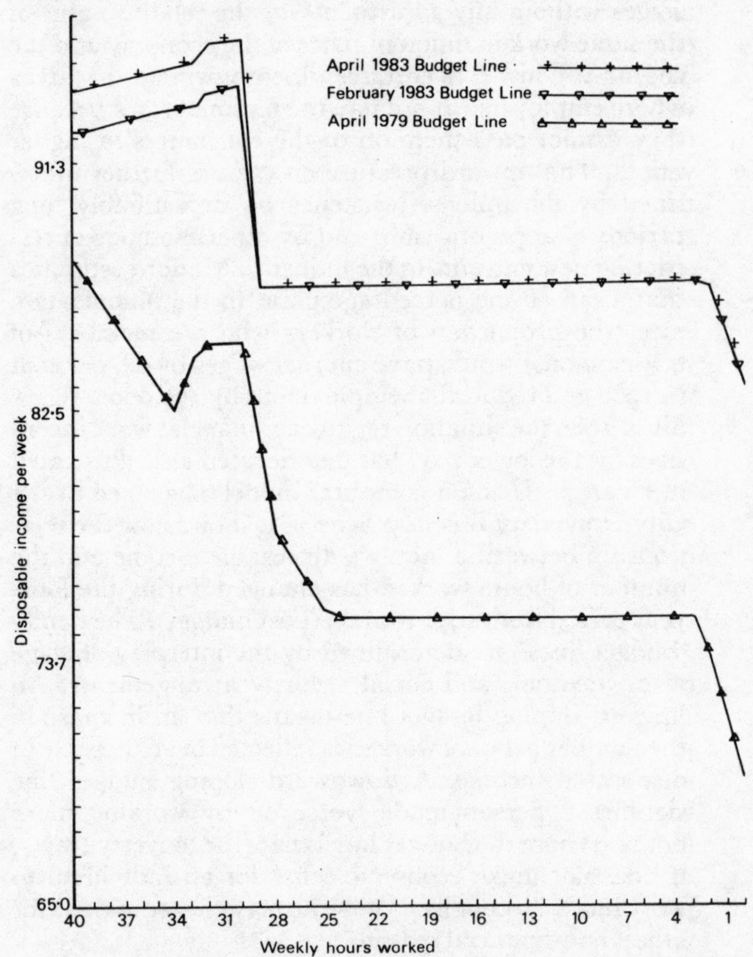

Supplement and housing benefits after thirty hours a week, has made work *less* rewarding financially for low-paid workers. The present flat-rate benefit system also reduces wage flexibility: when wages fall, benefits do not fall in like proportion and act as a floor below wages. Unlike those in many other European countries, benefits in the UK do not vary with wage levels. Belgium also operates a flat-rate benefit system with similar effects on the behaviour of wages and unemployment. The use of benefit ratio ceilings is widespread in Europe: in Germany total net social security benefits are fixed at 68 per cent of previous net earned income during the first year out of work, falling to 58 per cent after that; in Italy the ratio is two-thirds indefinitely; in Denmark the standard ratio is set at 80 per cent, as well as there being a maximum absolute amount.

Minford estimates that if a ceiling of 70 per cent were established in this country, unemployment would be reduced by three-quarters of a million over five years, with nearly £4 billion contributed to the PSBR, allowing tax cuts to be made to ameliorate the distributional consequences of this measure. By contrast, Minford estimates that a 10 per cent rise in real benefits would, at current unemployment levels, raise unemployment by nearly the same amount. In the absence of a fully operational negative income tax system, further measures that have been suggested to reduce the high marginal tax rates on the lower-paid include the raising of tax thresholds and child benefits, the computation of Family Income Supplement on the basis of net income (instead of on gross as at present), and the abolition of means-tested benefits in kind and their replacement with a more generous FIS.
(Minford, ibid., pp. 9–59.)

24. According to the 1982 General Household Survey [HMSO], 10 per cent of the registered unemployed were not looking for work. Many may have thought it a waste of time to search, but others may have been hoping for the opportunity of an increase in income by finding a 'good' job, particularly women, who make up two-thirds of those not looking for work but still on the register. This lack of urgency confirms the findings of a study in 1973 (W. W. Daniel, *A National Survey of the*

Unemployed, PEP (now PSI), October 1974) which showed that 12 per cent of the unemployed did not intend to find a job and a further 10 per cent claimed it was not important for them to find work. A similar conclusion has been reached in France and the USA. (Miller and Wood, op. cit.)

25. The most optimistic forecast for unemployment, by the City University Business School, projects that *if* the labour market were allowed to operate freely, the level of unemployment could fall below 2½ million in 1985 and to under 2 million by the beginning of the next decade. This means that even under the most favourable labour market conditions, 7 per cent of the working population would remain unemployed.
26. J. M. Keynes, *The General Theory of Employment, Interest and Money*, Macmillan, London, 1936, p. 374.
27. Many of the arguments in this chapter are developed in greater depth by the moral philosopher, H. B. Acton, in his *Morals and Markets*, IEA with Longmans.

5. THE IDEOLOGICAL DIMENSION

1. Max Weber, op. cit., pp. 20–2.
2. In particular: Milton Friedman (with the assistance of Rose D. Friedman), *Capitalism and Freedom*, University of Chicago Press, Chicago, 1962; Milton and Rose Friedman, *Free to Choose: A Personal Statement*, Secker & Warburg, 1980.
3. Carl Becker, *The Heavenly City of the Eighteenth Century Philosophers*, Yale University Press, London, 1932, pp. 47–58.
4. Quoted in Carl Becker, op. cit., pp. 51–2.
5. Quoted in Carl Becker, op. cit., p. 52.
6. Holbach, *Système social*, 1, 58, quoted in Carl Becker, op. cit., pp. 52–3.

7. David Hume, *Dialogues Concerning Natural Religion*, quoted in Carl Becker, op. cit., pp. 55–6.
8. Carl Becker, op. cit., p. 53.
9. Isaac Newton, *Principia Mathematica*, quoted in Carl Becker, op. cit., p. 57.
10. Ibid.
11. Alexander Pope, *Essay on Man*, 1, viii; ix, 1733, in *The Complete Poetical Works of Alexander Pope*, Crowell, New York.
12. Adam Smith, op. cit., p. 111.
13. Ibid., p. 62.
14. Ibid., p. 364.
15. Ibid., pp. 475 & 477.
16. Charles Darwin, *On the Origin of Species by Means of Natural Selection*, (1859), Penguin, 1968, p. 68.
17. H. Spencer, *Social Statistics*, D. Appleton & Co., New York, 1864 (1831), p. 42.
18. A. Marshall, op. cit., p. 42.
19. William Graham Sumner, *The Challenge of Facts*, p. 67, quoted in Richard Hofstadter, *Social Darwinism in American Thought*, Beacon Press, 1955, p. 58.
20. Quoted in Richard Hofstadter, op. cit., p. 45.
21. Milton Friedman, op. cit.; F. A. Hayek, *The Road to Serfdom*, Routledge & Kegan Paul, 1962; Hayek, *Law, Legislation and Liberty: A New Statement of the Liberal Principles of Justice and Political Economy*, Routledge & Kegan Paul, 1973–9; Ayne Rand, *The Fountainhead*, Signet Books, 1943; Rand, *We the Living*, Signet Books, 1936, 1959; Rand, *Atlas Shrugged*, Signet Books, 1957.
22. Milton Friedman, *Capitalism and Freedom*, University of Chicago Press, Chicago, 1962, p. 12.
23. Nietzsche, in W. G. Sumner, *What Social Classes Owe to Each Other*, p. 73, quoted in Richard Hofstadter, op. cit., p. 38.
24. H. Spencer, op. cit., pp. 414–18, quoted in Richard Hofstadter, op. cit., p. 41.
25. H. Spencer, op. cit., pp. 79–80, quoted in Richard Hofstadter, op. cit., p. 40.

6. THE CHALLENGE FOR BUSINESS

1. Richard Tanner Pascale and Anthony G. Athos, *The Art of Japanese Management*, Penguin.
2. Thomas J. Peters and Robert H. Waterman, *In Search of Excellence*, Harper & Row, New York, 1982.
3. Andrew M. Pettigrew, 'The creation of organisational cultures', a paper presented to the Joint EIASM–Dansk Management Centre Research Seminar, Copenhagen, 18 May 1976, p. 11.
4. Joanne Martin, 'Stories and scripts in organisational sellings', Research Report No. 543 (rev.), Graduate School of Business, Stanford University, July 1980, p. 3.
5. Philip Selznick, *Leadership and Administration: A Sociological Interpretation*, Harper & Row, New York, 1957, p. 28.
6. Thomas Watson Jr, *A Business and its Beliefs: The Ideas that Helped Build IBM*, McGraw-Hill, New York, 1963, pp. 4–6.
7. Pascale and Athos, op. cit., p. 49.
8. Pascale and Athos, op. cit., p. 193.

INDEX